Merry Christmas 2020

R.

GROUSE
COUNTRY

12/2/2020

For:
Mitchell —
These stories are all true
and your friend Randy Havel
was part of many. Heed what he
pays, as he is a first rate guy.
May your covers be full of birds
Best Wishes
Art Wheaton

GROUSE COUNTRY

Gunning with the Old Pats Society

By Art Wheaton

Published by
Peter E. Randall Publisher
Portsmouth, NH
2017

ISBN 13: 9781937721497
Library of Congress No. 2017944932

Published by
Peter E. Randall Publisher
5 Greenleaf Woods Drive U102
Portsmouth, NH 03801
www.perpublisher.com

Additional copies may be purchased from:
Strcamwood, Inc., 47 Grove Road, Forest City, Maine 04413

The following articles were previously published.
"A Gun, A Dog and a Long Time Ago" original published in *Double Gun Journal*
Others published in *Ruffed Grouse Society Magazine*, some unpublished

Author takes literary license with the words grouse, partridge, pa'tridge, or pat'ridge in the text. "When I refer to Grouse it's in recognition of the elevated significance of the bird to many, as in Mr. Grouse, king of the upland game birds. It is usually called partridge in New England, but local pronunciation has been modified by region. While pa'tridge tends to give it DownEast flavor, sounding like pah'ridge, the name pat'ridge is what my dad and others called them with emphasis on Pat, as in The Old Pats Society. Remember, we are country folks."

To my wife, Doris, who tolerated my many hours at the keyboard trying to put words together and my October disappearances into the covers for the necessary research, while the plants awaited holes, the grass grew higher, and garage clutter stayed secure.

The Old Pats Society

Earl G. Larson   1979 ★
Tom Larson   1979
L. E. "Chuck" Mosher Jr.
    "The Reverend Leroy"   1979
Vic Romano   1979
Ken "The Good Doctor"
    Waite Jr.   1979 ★
Art Wheaton   1979
Randy "The Great Morel" Havel   1980
Ken Berger   1986
J. Scott Hanes   1986
Rick Robison   1986
Pete Jackson   1987
Roger Lowell   1987
Kurt Nelson   1987
Ken Waite III   1989
Jerry Havel   1992
Ed Rossi   1992
Jon Foster   1994
Todd Lowell   1994

Lance Wheaton   1994
Shane Wheaton   1994
James Baker   1997
Tim McCormack   1997
Captain James Ryan Jr.   1997
Matt Hanes   1998
Bill Hamilton (Honorary)   2000
Brad Hanes   2001
Paul Bergere   2006
Parker Havel   2007
Parker Robison   2007
Allan Swanson   2011
Matt Ambrose   2012
Charles Stump   2012
Fred Stump   2012
David Larson   2014
Vinny Guglielimo   2015
Tim McKelvey   2016

★ deceased

Contents

Contents

Tom Beecham signed on in 1971 to what turned out to be nearly
three decades of painting Remington Calendars, creating a total of
348 images. His only self-portrait, in 1985, graces this cover.

Art Wheaton collection.

Foreword

Over the years, grouse and woodcock hunters have reveled in stories from those who devoted their writing talents to the king of upland gamebirds. Men like Burton Spiller, William Harnden Foster, and the ultimate storyteller, Gene Hill, have educated, entertained, and informed generations of sportsmen, especially those who were fortunate enough to be introduced to their magic by caring fathers and grandfathers. In a sport where seasons are too short and the time spent waiting for the next opening day much too long, crafted stories from latter-day writers like George Bird Evans, Steve Smith, Tom Davis, and Art Wheaton bridge the gap of "the long season between seasons."

Growing up in rural New Hampshire, my passion for hunting and fishing was always fueled by the next edition of *Sports Afield* and Cory Ford's column, *The Lower Forty.* His fictional town, Hardscrabble, sounded just like mine, and the characters that sat around the cracker barrel in the general store every fall were my family, friends, and the men I wanted to grow up to become! Years later, when Ford was asked if his characters were real, he said, "the Lower Forty is any circle of old friends who have hunted together in the cold, and fished in the rain, and shared the same memories over the years." The stories in the pages of this collection will take you to the places and times of your own special memories.

Art Wheaton's journey to outdoor writer evolved from sixty years as a registered Maine guide in Forest City, Maine, sharing stories from the square stern of a Grand Laker Maine Guide Canoe. In between those years and contributing to his evolution came marriage into the Jalbert family, whose long traditions of woodsmen, guides, hunters, and fishermen on Maine's famous Allagash River are legendary. His willingness to walk any grouse cover he could find from Washington County, Maine, and New Brunswick to Minnesota, and a long career as a senior executive with Remington Arms Company made writing a natural transition. That life-long passion for partridge (or pat'ridge) and woodcock, coupled with the memories made during his years as the unofficial chairman of *The Old Pats Society*, whom you will soon meet, makes it easy to see the inspiration for his outdoor stories. He has a connection to the glorious fall season, and he has the refurbished L. L. Bean boots and Filson brush pants to back it up.

In the chapter entitled "The Good Doctor," Art points out that "one doesn't make old friends," but his warm, often humorous yet true stories will remind you that hunting grouse and woodcock with good friends behind stylish pointers and setters may just be a great place to start the process!

L. E. Chuck Mosher, aka, The Reverend Leroy
Old Pat's Society Member

The Peters Cartridge Company 1928
image believed to be Count Gladstone IV
Art Wheaton collection

Watercolor by author's mother, Ruth E. Wheaton,
featuring Parker 20 gauge Trojan in Chapter 1.

Grouse Country

My interest in grouse hunting, hunting and fishing in general, began as part of a way of life. Grandfather, Arthur R., guided sportsmen before Maine guide licensing was required in 1897, then for forty years until his death in 1938. Woodie (1909–1990), my dad, since the age of fourteen and for sixty-eight consecutive years, was also a registered Maine guide, guiding sportsmen "from away," many guests of Weatherby's Camps in Grand Lake Stream, Maine, our home, as well as hunters who came to his own "Grand Lake Brook" camp.

Then in 1952, Ruth and Woodie built their own sporting camp, Wheaton's Lodge & Camps, in Forest City, Maine. They raised three boys; Lance, Dale, and yours truly; all finding themselves glued to the stern seat of a Grand Laker canoe while in their teens, working as chore boys then unofficial guides until license age. At that time, the local game warden had to sign-off on my competence, so at sixteen, college fund accumulation began. I still guide fisherman today but glorious October is mine.

Grouse and woodcock hunting began as a game of stealth, shot shells were purchased "by the each"…a full box was solid gold and table fare always the goal. Then, after repeated roars of flushing birds, I learned a refined taste for the excitement, skill, dog-work, and artillery selection—wingshooting was the pinnacle of satisfaction and reward. The deep and lasting value of camaraderie, acquisition of classic sporting art images, and a deep appreciation and respect for the birds elevated the passion to new heights. Along this wonderful journey, I have concluded that a miss may even be more memorable than a hit. While many gunners may not readily admit to such evolution, I now find as much pleasure with someone else's success, especially a newcomer's, as with my own.

Life deals us many hands, some good and some not so, but with a six-month's National Guard assignment beginning in the sands of Ft. Dix, NJ, and the fortunate meeting of another soldier, Ken Waite Jr., a summer employee of Remington Arms Company, Inc., the mesh of our keen interests in hunting and fishing, the outdoors, and his connections within the company, resulted in my same employ for some forty years and a deep and wonderful friendship of fifty.

Through the years, Octobers were filled with grouse and woodcock adventures in Connecticut, Maine, Minnesota, Wisconsin, Michigan, and Canada, remembered well by a fair amount of blue sky around flushing birds. Seriously, a few did have bad luck, in all sorts of cover, from early fall through the snows of winter, building a resume of hits and misses, as well as many experiences with dogs, some poor, some good, a slim few very good, and one of the finest English Setters, "Woodrow," I have ever seen. We "touched off" with a variety of guns, from Model 1100 auto-loaders, 870 pump action, Model 32 over-unders, and side-by-sides like L. C. Smith, Fox Model B, Ithaca and Parker, settling in and finally attached to the hip with what Peter Johnson calls, America's finest shotgun. First Parker 12s, then 20s, finally settling on the 28 gauge. Maybe gray hair, hills seemingly steeper, brush thicker, and slowing of the step contributed to the desire for lightweight carry.

Admittedly biased from my employment, the great old 1100 20s were the staple of my arsenal, with an 870 on occasion, and the only O/U acceptable was the veritable Model 32 that we called the "brush-buster." Influenced some by the American sporting prose of Spiller, Ford, and Foster (who each carried a Parker), by its solid legitimacy and acceptability of use due to Remington's purchase of Parker in 1934, and by our concluding that a gun with an American soul should be the first choice for America's greatest game bird, it became a regular companion.

My interest in a Parker started with a 12-gauge 30" VH full and full duck gun once belonging to an uncle, my grandfather's VH 16 choked mod full, then my very first grouse gun, the little Trojan 20, "choked open and opener" of "A Dog, a Gun, and a Long Time Ago," to a well-worn, silver receiver VHE 20, cylinder and cylinder, and now a wonderful little Parker 28-gauge skeet gun with skeet chokes, that on a lucky day came out from under a bed and landed in my lap. Less weight, quick handling, and no need to connect on each shot with advancing age, it has become my favorite of all time. Once in a while the birds fly into the pattern of Remington STS sporting clays, hard shot, #8s a best-kept secret for a superb grouse and woodcock load. That little 28 has been a regular part of the party, tolerated a great many of my stories, rested nearby during evening libation-fueled memories, and has been treated with the greatest of care. I am sure you have that special gun which gives you similar pleasure and has a ranking space in your cabinet or safe.

Most grouse and woodcock gunners take pride in a favorite gun, no matter the brand, action, or characteristics, be it their first gun, one with provenance handed down in the family, one that has proven success as it points where you are looking, or one with a special story of acquisition. A gun becomes an old friend and regular part of the uniform. Guns are to be enjoyed in a host of ways. Like a special lady, their preference is in the eyes and arms of the beholder, to be cherished, cleaned and oiled, viewed, admired, and shown to our friends. I enjoy guns—the instruments of our orchestra, both yours and mine!

For many years with public relations and marketing responsibilities for America's Oldest Gunmaker, and as an advertiser, the gamut of outdoor hunting magazines arrived each month, stacked high, lining our advertising offices. Just pick one out to your liking. The old standbys of *Outdoor Life* and *Field & Stream* were challenged by vertical and species-specific books. Content, writing styles, and subjects let a reader gravitate to personal preferences. Along with a growing gunning library, having acquired and read many books on grouse and woodcock, and having read hundreds of stories, I probably, maybe mistakenly, concluded I might just be able write a story. Fast forward to retirement, a bit more time, and love of the game; and on a lark I connected with the Executive Director of the Ruffed Grouse Society and began a regular column.

So, the journey began, crafting some of what we in the industry loosely called "whack and stack" pieces. The cover, the dog, the shot, and filling the bag, you have read the same. Then, while contemplating another submission, I realized, there's a great deal more to grouse and woodcock hunting than just pulling the trigger. I began to tap a growing resume, a menu of individual and group escapades centered around the endless adventures of our "Old Pats Society" and the characters involved. Disenchanted at times—I'm not really a writer you see, Gene Hill is a writer; Corey Ford is a writer; Burt Spiller, George Bird Evans, William Harnden Foster, and Ben Ames Williams are writers, just to name a few—but persistence prevailed. The journey continued, recalling the true stories banked in memory, and while the King's English was evasive at times, the unpublishable adjective descriptors more plentiful over libation, real facts and experience-based storytelling vs. fiction became the foundation. Leaving the "how to" for others, you all know how to do that, I found myself talking to kindred spirits, striving hard to draw the picture, build the bridge, touch the past or relate to the future about things, places, people, guns, dogs, birds, and times…those meaningful times, those memories and seemingly little things that enrich our sporting life with remembrance and reward, all that have had lasting importance to me.

Hopefully in some small way one of these little stories is meaningful to you, brings back a point in time, gives you pause to think and put new meaning to your own trips afield, accompanies your quiet time in the den looking at the things you hold dear, and persuades you to buy just one more gun, a new dog, and schedule another trip you've been putting off. Take and expose that new recruit along with your special friends so a new generation may find the true value in this sport of kings. It is why we do what we do, as all too quickly we find more good covers behind us than ahead of us.

Good hunting,

Art Wheaton
Old Pats Society
Forest City, Maine

Ralph Squier and "Doc," Ken Waite Jr.,
Art Wheaton with Springer Spaniel "Ike"
and Parker Trojan 20 gauge, Fairfield
County Fish and Game, circa 1968

Art, "Ike", and Parker VH 12 after duck
hunt on "Nell's Island", Housatonic
River, Connecticut, circa 1966

Christmas with Doris, my new bride,
and new dog "Ike", circa 1965

"Ike's" first winter at our cottage, Fairfield
County Fish and Game, Walker Hill Road,
Newtown, Connecticut, circa 1965

A Gun, a Dog, and a Long Time Ago

H e called me one day to ask, "Are you interested in a dog?" A dog was a bird dog in this case and I said, "We would love to have one."

Earl furthered, "A friend of mine passed away and the family wants to find a good home for his Springer Spaniel."

Earl Larson was a man of character, a "Remington Man" in those days, whose word you could take "to the bank." Arrangements were made for my new bride and me to drive from our home in Sandy Hook to Fairfield, Connecticut, on Sunday to pick up the dog.

That sunny fall day in 1965, we arrived to meet "Ike," a friendly black and white Springer Spaniel, and while getting acquainted with him over small talk in their kitchen, I asked, "Did Mr. have any guns?" "Yes," his daughter said, "let me get them." She soon produced a Beretta O/U Silver Snipe and a Parker 20-gauge Trojan.

Newly married with a bank account in name only, no washing machine or dryer, and clean clothes courtesy of the local laundromat, I boldly offered $200 for the gun, the sum total of cash wedding gifts in our collective wallets and representing one third of my monthly salary. The deal was struck!

Somebody asked me years later, "Why didn't you buy the Beretta?" The simple answer was that we were broke!

That treasured little 20 gauge frequented many grouse covers of Connecticut and the club grounds of Fairfield County Fish & Game, maybe not feared by the bird population, but at least acknowledged. At the ripe old age of twenty-four, it was strong medicine to own a Parker.

Upon close inspection, I suspected the barrels with their rather uncommon rib extension had been cut to 26" somewhere along its journey, but otherwise, it was a standard, well-used Parker Trojan 20 with splinter forend, double triggers, dog's head butt plate and pistol grip sans the Parker cap. The pride of owning a Parker 20 inched up a notch when my first grouse crosser, from right to left, met his demise.

The following summer, I ventured again into the dangerous territory of unfunded liabilities. Somebody was driving from Bridgeport, Connecticut, to Ilion, New York, and would deliver my gun to Larry Del Grego Sr., an old Parker/Remington gunsmith specializing in Parker and Remington Model 32 over and under shotguns.

After careful evaluation, his correspondence dated July 25, 1966, outlined recommended work, which included: polishing and re-browning the barrels, over boring (which would add a tiny bit of choke in cylinder bore guns and is sometimes referred to as jug choking), new ivory beads, opening the chambers for 2 ¾-inch shot shells, case coloring, new screws, and the fitting of a new stock for a special price of $171.50. The estimate, as some would say, was "more money than God" and eclipsed my requested $150 ceiling. When the gun came back and the press release reached the war department, my world would momentarily come to an end; but I survived the verbal flogging!

That little gun resided comfortably with me, enjoying combat with grouse and woodcock each fall until February 23, 1971, when Larry Del Grego Sr. again was called upon to install a new front ivory bead sight. An attempt to fit a mongrel set of barrels was discouraged.

Once more in 1978, the old Trojan made another trip to the hospital. While taking the gun from its case in the back of my station wagon during an October grouse hunt in northern Minnesota, my heart sank when I found the stock broken at the wrist.

Dollar signs once again flashed across my mind. So back it went to Larry. His letter of December 26, 1978, inflicted the expected pain to fit a new stock with 14" length of pull, 1½"-drop at the comb, 2½"-drop at heel and standard pitch. But alas, I had also discovered a couple of surprise dings, and a very slight bulge near the muzzle of the left barrel, all repairable to the tune of $359.00. My investment in 1965 of $200 had blossomed to $750.30 plus postage. By today's standard, maybe not much, but in those days a solid hit on the grocery money. Nevertheless, it came back in fine shape to partner with me again in the covers of Minnesota, Wisconsin, and Maine.

My attachment to this Parker 20-gauge Trojan grew from the coverts we shared, memories of that wonderful little Springer Spaniel, the friends we made, and the cherished trips we shared. Not unlike the "runt of the litter," that nobody wanted, but with solid genes that showed up at maturity to become a fine bird dog, old serial number 179,331 settled in as part of the family, maybe because of "Ike," maybe because of it being my first Parker 20, or maybe because it is a staunch reminder of the "no washing machine period" of our lives.

I bought one of those classic old leather lace-up boots, seemingly no longer available these days, which gave the stock just a tad more length. That boot became a part of the gun's uniform and it is worn proudly as a battle badge often used on guns from a long time ago.

We lost "Ike" in a strange way, a long time ago. He was left to curl up on our porch and stay home while we were away for a day. He was not there to greet us when we returned and our hearts ached for many long years. I found his collar one day, but nothing else, in a grassy field on Fairfield County Gun Club grounds. In the very same field he flushed that first cock pheasant I quickly dispatched for his retrieve in 1965. There were no other clues to "Ike's" disappearance, but to this day we have guilt about the loss of that fine little dog.

Now forty-five years later, courtesy of the Parker Gun Collectors Association, I know this old gun was ordered indeed a long time ago on 7-15-1919 by J. P. Daunrflser, 19 Warren St., New York City, with 28" barrels, along with six others of the same grade and some V Grades.

According to "The Parker Story," the concept of a Trojan grade material-ized in 1912 with a rib extension (sometimes confused with a doll's head on all grades above the base Trojan). About 1920 the extension was elimi-nated, so it is likely this 20 Trojan was built near the end of production for Trojans with an extended rib. Trojans are more commonly found without this extended rib.

For fifty-two years I have been reminded with some degree of frequency, almost always in mixed company, of that long ago monetary sacrifice, in lieu of a washing machine and dryer. But I will say unequivocally that my investments in the form of modern washing and drying equipment for the same period has significantly eclipsed the price of that old Parker. And my memory is refreshed each time a new "digital front loader washer and dryer" hits the market. Let that be a lesson to you gun buyers; such memo-ries are likened to a steel trap.

Insuring that this wonderful little Parker would stay in my family and be used one day by grandson Tyler, on December 25, 2003, the 20, in a fitted leather case, embroidered with the words "To Holly from Dad," that Trojan became a Christmas gift to my daughter. Included for posterity are all the repair letters from Larry Del Grego Sr. & Son that accompany my penned letter with full details of when and how the gun was acquired with "Ike."

One glorious October day in Maine, I posed the Old Trojan with a woodcock who "zigged when he should have zagged." At my request, my mother captured the photo in the watercolor included here as a frontispiece. That special watercolor painting is now part of the saga of old 179,311 and of a life now departed; January 12, 2011, at ninety-four-years young.

We are only stewards of these materialistic implements, but the recorded provenance may someday warm the heart of a grandchild's inquisitive mind, "I wonder how Grampy got this little gun?" Then the cycle will begin anew, hopefully, knowing a sentimental story from a long time ago may afford greater pleasure for another lifetime.

Parker 20 gauge Trojan with leather boot

Art and "Spot," first English Setter

Hell, It Might Just as Well Have Been an Elephant!

M y passion for hunting ruffed grouse—or "pa'tridge" as we say in Downeast Maine—came naturally. It was kindled one blue-sky October afternoon around 1954, when, summoning the courage, all the time, thinking about that trail up Daugherty Ridge, I asked, "Dad, can I take a gun and hunt up behind the house?"

He looked at me and thought a moment.

"You can take that pump gun," he said, pausing. "But I want you to be very careful and you have to hunt alone—no chums." He was insistent: "I don't want any of your friends going with you." This was the rule. He laid it down in such a tone of voice that there was no doubt he really meant it. I could have permission to hunt for the first time with a gun but safety came first. Dad grew up with guns and hunting, became a Maine Guide when he was fourteen, as was his father, so he knew well the seriousness of it all.

I quickly climbed the creaking wooden stairs from the kitchen to the spare closet and little gun cabinet where Dad kept his deer rifle, a Remington Model 14 in 32 Remington Special; a Lefever 12-gauge Nitro Special, and an old, hand-me-down, Winchester Model 97 pump-action duck gun. Heart beating right through my shirt, I took out the plain-barrel 30-inch full-choke Winchester with the faded bluing and brought it downstairs.

"Here's a few shells," Dad said, reaching into the old shell bag on the top shelf in the hall closet where he kept his H&R Model 999 22, compass, and hunting knife. He handed me three or four blue smooth paper Peters and green, ribbed Remington Express size 5 chilled shot. I was outside quickly, storm door rattling behind me, the old worn pump gun heavy in my skinny arms, chest puffed just a mite with teenage pride, crunching my way through the bright yellow and red leaves up that old trail behind the house.

As a country boy growing up during the 1940s and 50s in the village of Grand Lake Stream in Washington County, Maine, guns were part of every-day life. Venison, partridge, and ducks were common table fare. They supplemented the grocery budget as they had done in Dad's family. Expensive shotgun shells and rifle cartridges were meant to bring home game. The local Pine Tree store sold shotgun shells "by the each"; we didn't waste them.

Hurrying home from school each day left just enough light for about an hour to quietly ease along those beech- and maple-lined trails filled with crisp dry leaves in hopes of catching a pa'tridge, as we say, gritting in the road, or feeding on beechnuts in the leaves. Youth brings 20-20 eye-sight and topnotch hearing, and those keen senses allowed me to distin-guish a squirrel from a partridge rustling in the leaves. The plan on those fading, sunny afternoons, sneaking along, peering through openings in the heavy leaf cover, was to slip up on an ol' "biddy" looking for grub just before nightfall and quickly level a charge of fine shot in her direction in hopes of a pat'ridge supper.

My very first success was on that first day he let me take the Winchester. It was a nice gray bird that had filled her crop with beechnuts and hopped up on an old rotted stump to brag about it. She would make that "twit, twit" sound, cocking her head from side to side, tail turned up, tuned to danger. Her bright day then turned into a stroke of bad luck. Before her final alarm went off, I had sighted down the plain barrel of the duck gun, thumbed the outside hammer back from the half-cock position, and let fly.

Hell, it might just as well have been an elephant!

Proud like a rare *A* on my report card, I picked up my trophy and beat a hasty retreat home, not even thinking of trying to find another. Showing Dad that I could find and bag a bird on my own was big medicine.

That autumn afternoon started my lifelong love of grouse, as I later heard dignified folks "from away" call this king of upland game birds. Today, he is no longer bushwhacked—at least not by me. The distinct smell of a fired paper shotgun shell, or the aroma of age old Hoppe's No. 9 Bore Solvent is as keen to the senses today as it was long ago. So began the evolution and education of an upland bird hunter that has lasted all these past fifty-plus years, hunting them in many of their haunts across this great country.

Tom Larson, Tim Martin, Earl Larson,
Ken Waite Jr., Chuck Mosher, 1979

Art Wheaton, Tom Larson, Ken Waite Jr., Earl Larson, 1979

Why, We're "The Old Pats Society"

Charles E. Gillham once wrote a *Field & Stream* story titled, "Bird Hunting with Colonel Sheldon." Gillham quoted a letter from Colonel Harold P. Sheldon, author of the Tranquility series:

Dear Charley,

    I am preparing to leave for Vermont on Monday. Reports have it that woodcock are trampling down the farm crops up there, stealing lambs, colts, and calves. In three instances woodcock have carried off infants, diapers and all, to their nests high among the crags of the Green Mountains. Grouse, too, are present in great numbers and flying at velocities hitherto unknown. They have cut communication lines in several places, and our unfortunate countrymen are in a state of siege—subsisting miserably upon a diet of cob-smoked ham, bacon, blueberry pie, turnips, squash, McIntosh apples, maple syrup, and rum.

    Radio communications have been cut off, but a station in Berne, Switzerland, picked up an appeal evidently sent by the Governor of Vermont as follows: "Where in hell is Sheldon? In God's name, send Sheldon."

My passionate plea from Minneapolis, one evening in 1977, burned up the wires. "Good thing, it wasn't a party line," I thought.

I first *beamed up* my long-time good friend, Ken Waite Jr. in Monroe, Connecticut, expressing the excitement about a recent grouse hunt I had been on, just north of the Twin Cities. With tempered, yet pent-up enthusiasm over the phone, finally I said to Ken, "I have never seen such a hatch of grouse in my life." That's a pretty strong stuff for this Yankee, who grew up in the heart of Maine's historic grouse and woodcock coverts. No need for much coaxing, Ken found room in his schedule and our little party gathered, then took to the north country, he with his old Remington Model 32 and I with the Parker, a 12 gauge that was rescued from the used and abused rack and reconditioned by Larry Del Grego Sr. The thought of good grouse gunning had included more friends: Tom Larson and his dad, Earl, Vic Romano; Pete Jackson and his dad, fondly called The Admiral; and Chuck Mosher. With guns cased and brush clothes in our duffels, we piled into my station wagon, to have some of the finest grouse and woodcock shooting we had ever experienced.

During those glorious days, decades ago in that northern tier of Minnesota, grouse seemingly were in every covert and the makings of the Old Pats Society band of grouse and woodcock hunters was born, the name coming along later.

At the time, "Lucy," my little English Setter bird dog, came into her own. The dry leaves on the ground made it difficult to get close to birds unless they holed up in the thick, low brush. The peak of the cycle resulted in many broods still intact. Often two and three birds flushed near each other. Sure, I've flushed grouse from the same brood before but not with the frequency of 1977. This trip was highlighted when Ken and I converged on a knoll and at the bottom were low, multiple clumps of berry bushes, grouse were flushing all around us. I don't even remember how many we killed on the trip. But at the end of that spectacular day we had limited out, with Ken killing four birds without moving his feet from that spot atop the knoll while I hunted the low ground, flushing birds toward him, a feat that has never been repeated, even though we have had many a great grouse and woodcock hunt together. Nothing matched the flush count and success ratio of that Minnesota adventure.

But it was two years later, in 1979, when our little gang of kindred spirits gathered one sunny noon for a tailgate lunch break in Wisconsin. The conversation turned toward suggesting a name for our little band of desperadoes. It seemed fitting to pin a label on such a dedicated lot of partridge hunters.

Our most senior statesman, Earl G. Larson, dressed in his wool red-checked shirt, fluorescent ball cap and vest, often with a Winston hanging from his lip, listened with interest. Earl was then Product Service Manager at Remington Arms Company, an excellent competitive skeet shooter with a slightly raspy voice often heard on the next field as he called "Pull!" for the high-house bird, then "Mark!" for the low-house. He was a prince of a man, a straight shooter, someone we all looked up to. Earl adjusted his horn-rimmed glasses and offered up immediately, "Why, we're the Old Pats Society." The name stuck!

Jim Baker & "Skye"

Shane & Art Wheaton with "Max"

Sweet Spots

F ind the groceries and generally you will find the birds.

Dad once told me when we were bass fishing, "Find the groceries [baitfish] and you'll find bass." That piece of advice works for partridge and woodcock hangouts.

I have found, there's *a cover within a cover*. Likened to the best place to hit a ball off a tennis racket, a baseball bat, or that layer of frosting in the center of a cake…it's a sweet spot.

One of our most important bird hunting assets is familiarity with the cover, gleaned from having hunted it with some frequency. It may all look the same along the edge and outside, but there are likely higher probability zones within the larger tract. A special reason for a wise old bird to be there can be an apple tree, thickets of berry bushes, or thornapples. Places where birds concentrate. So, play close attention to the food sources, also the underbrush, the escape routes, age of the birches, alders or whips. All are key components to bird concentration. Those smart old birds didn't just fall off the "turnip truck." They spend their lives avoiding hawks, owls, and other predators, fill their crops every day with vital daily nutrition, and survive by knowing, well, their own backyard. I mentally mark bird location on each flush and ask myself, "Why were they there?" Remembering their favorite lunch sites improves my success, as I don't just blunder into a cover. Knowing the location of those spots helps determine the best approach to outwit those smart old "biddies."

To me, this means just because you parked the truck handy to a cover in an easy turnout and the regular entry to a cover is likely adjacent, it sometimes is wise to walk to a different entry point, a spot on the back side and put yourself between the old growth and the early successional stuff.

"That cover looks good," commented one member of the "Old Pats Society" as we drove along a dusty back road. Looking to my right, there was evidence of an old woods road. It disappeared into the evergreens, along the edge of an old orchard bordered on one side by a fence on a side hill next to a farmer's field. Upon further inspection, it just did not look so inviting to me because it was an *old* cover. Nevertheless, we decided to give it a quick hunt. Gathering our dogs and gear, we departed the vehicle and commenced to ease into the open area, approaching a snarl of branches from old rotted apple trees and fallen alders. Some of those trees continued to bear fruit, but most of the crop lay on the ground.

"Mark!" called Ken. A bird flushed ahead. "Skye," Jim's English Labrador Retriever was on it. Jim fired as the bird cleared a near-dead, old apple tree. "Dead bird," hollered Ken and the Lab was off, coming back with a fine gray-phase bird. Not an attractive cover we agreed, but the rotting fruit on the ground was the magnet.

This place, not much on a scale of one to ten, always seemed to hold a bird or two in *exactly* the same place. Never down in the hollow where the old brook runs through, or close to the field where there's no "grub," but always where the remains of that old rotting orchard withered away on the side hill. It undoubtedly was the corner of an old farm and even after hunting deeper, around its edges and in adjacent areas, the apple trees have always proven to be the attractor, *the* "sweet spot" of this likely to be passed over cover.

Hunting with my son, I asked a homeowner if we could hunt the edge of a small field behind his house. We decided to work along the far side, hunting the transition area, where the thickets change to old pines and hardwood. We hoped this edge would produce a grouse near his escape route. A half hour was spent working this out, to no avail, then, at the far end, we turned one-hundred-eighty degrees and came back nearly parallel to our original route, but forty yards closer to the field edge. It became increasingly clear the thicker under-brush, with an occasional old apple tree and some bushes with an assortment of berries, could be promising. My little Setter began to lock up, then move ahead toward the open field. One could hardly see through the tight cover. We had a bird moving on the ground and she finally pinned it. There was no way out without it taking flight toward the field. A few steps more and I heard it flush.

"Mark," I hollered. My son Shane's Parker VHE 20 barked once. Above the alders, I saw the bird catapult to the ground. "Dead Bird," I called out. "Good shot." This bird broke up and out toward the open field, a big mistake because we had forced it away from its normal escape route and it became fully exposed as it took flight. Basically, we made the bird flush in a direction he would not have chosen.

This little cover showed us once again that the very *heart* of it was the most productive. It always seemed to contain one-to-three birds and maybe a woodcock. When we hunted it other times, that small center section of about fifty yards, right where the food and thickest cover were concentrated, always proved to be the sweet spot.

I remember another place woodcock seemed to patronize. A meandering cover, along the edge of a little road that ends abruptly in an opening, a place that is a little field now but may have been a sort of depot for logs that were brought to this central location. I usually hunt along the left side of the road, follow around the field about thirty yards in and gradually move deeper to the edge of a swamp. The telltale whitewash or splash is always solid evidence of woodcock usage, but in this case only occasional whitewash showed until one got closer to the swamp. This is quite typical for the little gentleman as he finds earth worms in the moist areas along the lowland. The reminder here is that all the cover should be hunted methodically, not avoiding the slopes and little road edge, but keeping in mind old beady eyes and his pals will most likely be along the edge of the swamp, glomming down worms and be-bopping along under a few little spruce trees. If it is a wet year, his lunch spots are more widely spread, but he will not find earthworms where the soil is acidic, where you see the moss and lichens. I find along the slope on the way out of this piece a likely place to find a grouse, especially on a sunny morning. Many trips through this cover have confirmed the preferred hangouts for that "country gentleman." I know how to hunt it and where lunch is usually served, and although the whole piece should be hunted, the "sweet spot" always proves to be the center of the action.

Although there are large, aged cutovers that have a wide dispersal of birds, I have found that many of the old covers I hunt have that "cover within a cover." Paying close attention to where you find and flush birds and to the time of day you find them there will suggest whether those same places remain a strong bet again. Watch their getaway routes and try a different approach when hunting the same place, forcing the birds to choose another less familiar route, thus to your advantage. Give those birds credit for locating the best places to eat, hide, get out of Dodge, or just play "cribbage."

Whether it is a sunny slope with a menu of delicious hors d'oeuvres or a dense little hideout, "sweet spots" are a solid part of my playbook of fall hunting.

The Reverend Leroy scores with a pair of cock.

Fred Stump, Jerry Havel, Tom Larson, and Brad Milne

"Lucy" in Minnesota

"Lucy" at her best

"Lucille"

Right from the start "Lucy" knew birds. This little Setter—mostly white with black ticking, with black ears, a black-and-tan eye patch on her right eye—had a loving disposition around the kids and would sneak right up on the sofa if given the chance. She immediately pointed a grouse wing in the back yard, was very "birdy" in that first cover, and handled quite well for a young dog. On point she had great style with a high head and a little sickle curl to her tail, not liked by trial folks.

One time in the cemetery cover, she went nuts with that first dose of hot scent and decided to take a tour of the back forty. In the next cover that day, she decided to go to the hill beyond and look over the scenery. And one winter she discovered rabbit tracks—fair game. She could track one with her nose convinced there must be a grouse at the end. The time she thought the adjacent covert was so much better than the one we were hunting, my raspy voice nearly gave out, hollering, "Come," and then, a more emphatic, "Come, you x#@*$+&!" Her selective hearing took over. All my commands, no matter the octave, were energy wasted.

At the top of her game, this little Setter was solid as a rock. I remember one fine October morning, as friends and I gathered around the tailgate of my old station wagon to case our guns and discuss our plan for the next cover, my friend raised his arm and said, "Hey, look over there; she's on point." "Lucy" was locked up solidly at the edge of the field. I thought, "So, you think 'Lucy' doesn't know what she's doing?"

"Lucy" came to me as a replacement. The first was Jack, a nice six-month-old Setter from Nancy Whitehead, then of New Hampshire. But some bad luck came our way when Jack developed a form of dysplasia. It was not a good day for the family. I called Nancy in New Hampshire.

"We have some bad news. Our vet says Jack's hip is not fixable."

Nancy was most understanding. "I have one Setter pup left that we had decided to keep," she said. "We'll send her as a replacement."

Good photos remain as lasting evidence capturing some of her spectacular moments. She shined and made me proud, the envy of all onlookers. Sometimes the gunner performed; other times he did not hold up his part of the bargain, but there was never a question of "Lucy's" scenting ability. This wonderful little Setter was the pride and joy of our family. A sensitive nose, great style, and some good bird sense personified her performance during the 1980s. She was a nice grouse dog, but alas, my lax training did not correct the faults. Isn't it amazing how smart one becomes over time, sort of like the kid who didn't realize how smart Dad was until the kid reached twenty-two?

Yes, I'll admit it, "Lucy" occasionally had a mind of her own and she exercised it from time to time. In those days, there were fewer electric collars; besides, she deserved to relax in the off-season, like me, looking ahead through the months to next September: Then I'll show how good a shot I am, and she'll be more careful in the coverts because of her greater maturity and experience. Then it dawned on me that the "Splendid Splinter" (Ted Williams) could not hit a home run every time. Hitting .400 came from practice, practice, and more practice. She would be a terrific bird dog.

Somewhere along the way "Lucy" got a little lax. Surely, it couldn't be my fault, especially my failure to correct those inconsistencies before they became serious, nor my being too busy to do some much-needed yard training. I began to take some friendly heat. Behind my back, whispers surfaced that were less than complimentary of my dog. With increasing frequency, the tag end of a conversation went like this: "Boy. I would have had a few more birds if we just could have kept 'Lucy' closer." Occasionally accolades were passed out for a staunch point and retrieve. Things were never perfect. Even so we shot many, many birds with her. But once in a while she would get crazy and hunt at her own pace, sometimes way off to my left or right, or too far out in front, especially after getting a real snoot full of woodcock scent or where a brood of grouse had been hanging out in a thicket. I had grown to accept those little imperfections thinking that a little re-training in the off-season would surely straighten her out.

Yes, more backyard training, that's the answer. No more putting up with her selective hearing. No sir, I thought, this is it. I've had it. She is going to pay attention or so help me! Just like a New Year's resolution—commitment, perseverance, and a strong resolve to get the job done.

Well, you can't train in the winter months. It's too cold. The best time to start is April or May. Somehow cultivating the garden slowed my start, and then the yard needed attention, from all the debris of winter. June will work out fine. Damn weather got so hot, so fast, a dog just can't scent in this weather. Same for July. With August came the sweltering heat. I've got to keep the dog inside till this weather cools off a bit. Too much pollen in the air, the ragweed is at its height and the foliage is too thick for good dog work. September will be just great for a tune up. Then came business assignments that took me out of town for a good part of the month.

Oh, my God, I thought. Next week we head out for the Old Pats Society annual gathering.

I would get her in the woods a few days ahead of time; it will take just a few reminders to bring her back in line. She is off, back in the coverts. A few corner patches, a strip of poplars, a well-defined cutover in among some older growth, and "Lucy" is doing well. We find a few birds and connect. What a great opening day! The woodcock are in, scent is strong, and most coverts have birds. Grouse are near the apple trees but not holding well and the cover is sparse at ground level. It's a good year for apples. Expectations are high.

The next day we find an old deserted farmland and "Lucy" is given an opportunity to shine. As we bust our way through the brush, she gets her first real dose of grouse scent. A brood of the year, not yet dispersed, gets surprised by her sudden arrival. The beeper begins that continuous beep, beep, beep. We know she is on point. A couple of birds get nervous and go quickly airborne, followed by our shots in rapid succession.

"Whoa, 'Lucy,' come around—come, come in here." She is in heaven hunting by herself, birds flushing in all directions. So, the holler-fest begins, "*singing to the dog like the field trialers*," to get her back near the guns. Everybody knows you must have a good strong voice to be a dog handler. She decides to try the next rise and the next hollow off to my left. I make an attempt to get close enough to intercept her and finally get a lead on her collar. Needless to say, the day has been severely interrupted. Back in camp, sarcasm is meted out with reckless abandon.

She's got a good nose and with a little yard training in the off-season she will be fine. I am determined.

November came. A select few of the Old Pats Society were a part of an annual sales meeting; we just happened to have the same employer. A great place to replay the hunt, show the pictures, and talk about new guns, improved choking, the right shells, and what we will do next October. We'll be in better shape then, buy new deerskin gloves to ward off the briars, spend quality time tuning up that grouse dog…you know how it goes. The plans, purchases, and expectations are all part of the lore. Getting ready for next year starts right after the last hunt.

At the closing session of our meeting, annual awards highlight the accomplishments of the prior year. Transfixed by the glow of a little Scotch, the accolades placed on many great sales accomplishments and typical closing remarks, I hear the country western band tuning up for the ending evening celebration.

And then, I recognized the background tune, one of Kenny Rogers's old favorites, then an announcement of a special award to Art Wheaton for—dog training. From the microphone: "We want to take this moment to identify one of our own, for his untiring efforts training his own bird dog and, by recognition of his peers, he is tops in this category." The music is just a little louder now. I hear more words from the podium: "For knowl-edge and leadership in training his dog we present him with this year's Top Gun award." With that, the whole congregation breaks out with a slightly less than harmonious chorus of, *"It's a fine time to leave me, Lucille…I will finally quit living my dreams."*

What can a good man do to reclaim his dignity?

"Lucy" was a fine bird dog. Really. I'm going to fix those guys! Just wait till they see what I do in the off-season with a little more basic yard work. They'll regret those words.

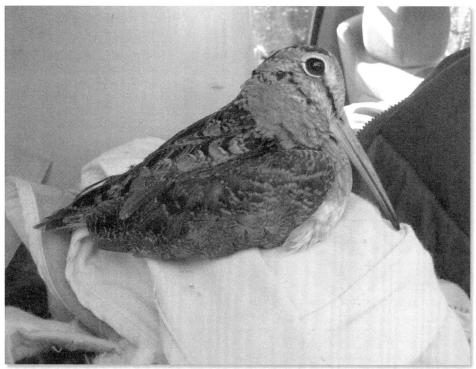

The eyes warm our heart.

Without woodcock our Octobers would be incomplete.

Driving with Miss Daisy

W oodcock are special!

"Mark!" hollered Randy, as a woodcock spiraled upward, just in front of his little Setter. It lifted, banked and flew, momentarily, parallel to the brook on our right; then veered sharply across the brook. I touched off!

Unfortunately, it fell on the other side. Now what? Without hesitation, the Setter plunged in, swam to the other side, nosed around a bit, located the bird and swam back, delivering it to hand.

But that wasn't all! As we pushed forward along the edge of the brook, unable to cross over, the cover ran out. A grouse appeared from nowhere, on our left, right out in the open, with afterburners lit for some distant destination. Randy took a snap shot and stoned the bird, downing it right in the open pasture. We will never know from where it came or what caused it to present such a clear shot…usually one that is missed.

George Bird Evans expressed his feeling for woodcock pretty well, "…after an October and a November that have been the first in my recent memory without woodcock, beyond a couple of afternoons that offered more than a lone shot over a point, I realize more than ever how barren an autumn would be without this lovely little bird."

Some of our finest gunning is on woodcock, leaving an album of great memories in the scrapbook of our mind. But with these challenging and exciting targets there will always be a feeling of reverence for this gentle, russet-colored little bird.

Opening that album from yesterday to the faded dog-eared snapshots from a glorious October day in the woodcock covers of northern Wisconsin, there were treasured images of this annual ritual. My gunning companion, Randy Havel, called "The Great Morel" (for morel mushrooms) by the Old Pats, and a friendly little ticked English Setter named "Crissy" spent a day not long enough. Both woodcock and mushrooms are delectable delights, it's all in the preparation.

This adventure began around Thorpe, Wisconsin, a wide spot off Highway 29, and home of the infamous Thorpedo Restaurant, so identified with a huge rocket sign that had no resemblance to a torpedo to me. The attraction thirty years ago was those grand tag alder covers nearby and a classic "Thorpedo" burger for midday sustenance.

Early on we found the birds spotty, as we sampled numerous covers, trying to find good rich, acid-free soil with telltale white wash. The hot spot turned out to be a little alder run bordered by a lazy meandering brook on one side and a cow pasture on the other. That busy English Setter quickened my pulse along with the frequent barking from Randy's Ithaca 20 bore Nitro Special. My old silvered receiver, Parker 20 chimed in, making music all afternoon, only interrupted by a monster whitetail that crashed out ahead, unexpectedly.

By late afternoon and in high spirits we decided to call it quits. I had tossed my hunting vest on top of the old wooden shell box in the back and headed home.

Soon a very strange sound was coming from the "way back," as my kids called it. The "way back" you know, is just out of arms-length from the disciplinarian in front seat.

The infrequent, muffled scratching sounded much like an ailing transmission, or was it simply a piece of brush dragging. It was intermittent, like a branch touching the road when my station wagon hit a bump. Or was it coming from the inside of the car?

I was paying more attention to Waylon and Willie than any other noises, but every once in a while this odd sound filled the void before

Willie launched into another old favorite. A look into the rearview mirror from time to time suggested nothing seemed out of order. Yet on one such glance, I thought I saw movement in my old hunting vest, or was it? No, must have been my imagination.

All of a sudden, there was rustling under or in the vest. "What the heck is that?" I thought. Then, before I could think much about it, the head of a woodcock popped out of my game pouch, rocking and reeling, shaking off a bad hangover. "Daisy" began to emerge carefully, showing more and more of herself, looking around, taking in the sights, yet unable to "walk the line" for a police officer inspection.

Like old George Carlin, the comedian who imitated alcoholic overindulgence, "Daisy" begins to bob and weave, dancing from one foot to the other across the top of my gear, sometimes sitting with a hiccup or two in contemplation of the next move. Soon she popped to the top of the rear seat and was prancing back and forth like a rooster on a fence. One could see the gradual improvement in her steadiness, a growing confidence in her stature, a bit more aggressive, braver, and surer of herself.

This little drama began to pick up tempo. From a hippity-hop dance, bobbing head and drunken stupor, I now observed a prancing, and stretching of the wings, sometimes using the wings for steadiness over a little crevasse. Having done guard duty walking back and forth across the seat back, interest in the side windows and adjacent ledge took on a new attraction. She began leaning against the windows and hopping along the ledge, followed by a short limp to the heap of hunting clothes and onto the other ledge and window, all the time, the action intensifying.

Now this charming little brown lady was gaining in spirit, energy, and stamina. I was enamored by the sun dance. During the short hops, her wing dragged noticeably along, reflecting the encounter with number 9 "chilled" shot.

"What to do now?" I thought. "Shall I stop the car and deal with 'Daisy'?" With a broken or damaged wing, there can be no alternative than to finish the job originally intended.

Finally home, I dropped the tailgate and peered into the big brown eyes of that wonderful little shaded brown colored bird who had somehow touched me. Right then, if I had had a choice, she would have been released back into a cover.

Next time you pick up one of these great birds, just take a look into those big bulging eyes. It is cause for strong reflection on "something of value."

It often takes an event like "Driving Miss Daisy" to become more intimate with a species, more genuinely interested in preserving the game and the sport for future generations. It left me forever with thoughts that a "woodcock limit" need not be filled to have the greatest day shooting. My appreciation grew for Gene Hill's poignant words, "I know that a woodcock I once saw years ago against the evening star has flown softly through evenings that I would have dreaded had I been alone without him."

John Gaskins and "Cali" in New Brunswick, retrieve of Charles' first grouse

Ken Waite Jr. and Vic Romano Jr., Minnesota 1980, comparing fans;
Scottish hats in style

Randy Havel and Art Wheaton at "The Honey Hole," Minnesota

Do You Remember...Old Pal

Do you remember, old pal, our chance meet? A most unlikely place, or was it: in Uncle Sam's barracks built on a sandy landscape far from our homes. We found brief Saturday afternoon respites in the written word of hunting and fishing. Those stories of inviting faraway places in *Outdoor Life* forever linked our lives.

Do you remember, old pal, when our headlights hit the whitecaps of the incoming tide and high wind at the boat ramp in the early morning hours. Our boat trailed behind, loaded with decoys, paddles, and surrounded with a reed blind. The night before we had worked hard in preparation. The incoming inclement weather pattern lined up perfectly for great duck hunting weather. But we just sat there, weighing the danger ahead against the excitement of the hunt. We talked it over, turned and went home, disappointed but alive; our good judgment prevailed while other more brazen hunters did not return.

Do you remember, old pal, the time we found that the crows were patronizing their familiar restaurant, the town dump. We slipped in before dawn and set out the slab-sided plywood decoys that we built ourselves. The wise old birds came in cautiously, with wings set, gliding carefully, some silent, some cawing to another. We were covered with our white sheets, hidden amongst the debris, the ground covered with a light new fallen snow. Soon the snow was littered with downed birds, frequently bloodied by a once angry raider who fell to a well-placed shot. All at once a local policeman showed up, parked his car and walked into the scene of the massacre. He looked up at the crow hanging in the tree, cawing for all its worth, thinking he was in Zulu land. Suddenly our friend Ralph asked him, "Can I help you?" The officer, one hand on his revolver, jumped, visibly surprised, and even though he heard the voice could not locate the source, until Ralph removed his sheet. "Do you have to make all the noise?" he said. "The neighbors are complaining."

Do you remember, old pal, the time you and "Pops" sent me up the mountain for a wise old white face buck and at the top, as he stared at me, the hammer fell but my gun did not fire. A likely story you said, but you knew he was there and chose to give me the first opportunity.

Do you remember, old pal, the time you, Ralph, and I, hunted grouse in the Naugatuck State Forest? Those were grand days but it seems like only yesterday. Long gone now is Chief, his big Setter dog, along with a cast of our companions: "Ox," "Pretty," "Doc," "Ike," "Lucy," "Ginger," and "Trimmer." Now the legs find those hills a bit steeper, logs higher, and the gun heavier, but those wonderful adventures of yesterday have deep meaning.

Do you remember, old pal, the time we hunted around Monroe, Connecticut, when the available land still had a few grouse and an occasional woodcock. The time we worked a cover off Lebanon Road and the great barred owl zoomed out of a tree, having just finished off a fine grouse, and you pulled the trigger, sending the marauder hurriedly away. And the little woodcock haunt at the end of Wheeler Road. And the Hammertown swamp where there were always a few birds. All gone now, succumbed to the bulldozer, housing and supposedly…progress.

Do you remember, old pal, the times in Minnesota? The grouse numbers were at their peak and in most covers we got great dog work. Our combined success was extraordinary, highlighted by you killing four successive grouse from a rise without moving your feet, while "Lucy" and I worked the heavy brush at the bottom…and from that time on we called ourselves "The Old Pats Society." That's when you missed the straightaway and we watched and cheered, never to be forgotten. That's when we "limited out," lined our birds on the barbed wire fence to brag, now a single or brace seems to be plenty.

Do you remember, old pal, the time on that frigid cold day with snow on the ground, we had that great hunt in the frozen swamp, dined in the station wagon and listened to Fran Tarkenton break new records, often between drooping eyelids and power naps.

Now, as the ravages of time leave their imprint, our occasions afield become fewer. Our routines include a trek daily to the post office box, taking out the old guns and cleaning them once again, looking at a few ragged old photos of days gone by, working on a good book from the stack on the nightstand or exchanging calls with a few cherished old friends. We recall with great fondness the memories, the good times we've had, the great shots we've made *and* misses, and we relive the old stories again and again. Now in the twilight of those grand old adventures of yesterday, I am reminded of the great fortune of finding a lifetime of friendship exploring those coverts together.

> And as the shadows grow longer for us, Old Pal,
> "I wish that we could live the old days over,
> Just once more.
> I wish that we could hit the trail together,
> Just once more.
> Say Pal, the years are slipping by,
> With many a dream and many a sigh,
> Let's chum together, you and I,
> Just once more."

Now the days of our prime are over. We look through our accumulation of prized possessions and decide each year that some things are just not as important as they were. In our youth, we once valued them so highly, now we search for a willing steward, hopefully a family member, to give them great care for another lifetime. In the end, it is not those totems that *really* matter; it is the good luck of having found a friend for a lifetime. You, my friend, old pal, are a true treasure who has provided me with such a rich and meaningful trip through these past fifty years.

I am reminded that with age comes wisdom. The wisdom of knowing there are some things one cannot recover from: the stone…after the throw; the word…after it has been spoken; and the time…after it is gone.

May you have the wisdom to recognize first, then treasure, the true fortune of an often rare and long-lasting friendship. It will make the trail of life wide, and well paved.

John Gaskins and "Molly" at Tomah

Art and "Molly" "the horse back cover"

Wilhelmina & Hamlet Wheaton, final rest

Wilhelmina (1844–1909) & Hamlet Wheaton (1842–1919),
(9th & 11th R.I. Vol Infantry, 3rd R.I. Vol Calvary)

The Old Place

Unless you know a little about its past and just how to find it, "The Old Place" doesn't exist.

Watch for a landmark when proceeding north on Route 1; there's an old house on the right that sets back from the road among those huge, overgrown maple trees. A once graceful, beautiful residence built right after the Civil War, it is now ramshackle, most windows broken out, rotted timbers, and gray, cracked-wood siding with weathered ornamental trim, secluded, but aging steadily, with a hint of grandeur situated upon that gentle rise. You are likely to drive right by it and not know there was even a house back there, except for what appears to be a dead-end driveway that is still discernable, only because the grass and weeds have a hard time growing in that sandy little space.

Once you pass that old house, quickly look left; the only clue from the tarmac is two metal posts with a couple of florescent tapes tied to a sagging cable across the last visible evidence of an old road. The entrance is heavily canopied in alders now; dandelions, a few buttercup wild flowers, clover, and tall grass fill in the center of those barely distinguishable tracks. One gets a sense of an old wagon track or might speculate this was a tote road used for a little wood cutting operation, but a few aged folks know better. In the late spring, when the vegetation is heavy and the alders are fully leafed-out, most of the evidence is in complete camouflage.

To start down this road, you must duck your head and walk fifty-feet in, where it becomes clearer and more distinct. It's the last gasp of a woodcock cover; no grouse. Large pine and spruce trees dominate the right-hand side and form an older forest, while the left has a lot of alders, an apple tree here and there, and when you ease along far enough you'll notice a few younger alders are growing along the edge of the remaining field. The very edge looks inviting for an occasional woodcock or two that might drop in hoping for easy grub. Under the sprinkling of little birches and alders at the field edge, the soil is free of acid, and worms do well in the fertile soil, while the rotting floor under the apple trees is full of twigs and moss. I always hope a few rotted apples will attract a grouse.

It is a nice short walk, cooled by the canopy. Just off to the left of this little road are the remains of an old rock foundation. Rusting barrels, pails, and cans are scattered around. The remnants of something that I could not identify lay rotting away; that apparatus of metal and wood leans against the rock work which is almost completely covered with grass and moss. The dog usually works around on this side as it looks more promising. He sometimes finds a little scent, but nothing to make him serious. I very much like that old homestead, have to give it a short hunt once a season, just so it's not forgotten. When the afternoon sun slips lower, casting a few shadows, "the old place" makes you wonder about those folks of yesterday, how the birds hung around that old farm, and what a place it must have been.

After passing remnants of a granite block foundation for another couple hundred feet, the cover gets a little better; then, at the field edge, the younger growth of birches, alders, and a few small fir and spruce look like a pretty setting for woodcock. I notice a bit of chalk spattered infrequently. We must then swing left or right along the old field for better chances. But a magnet pulls me straight ahead while the dog searches wider, hoping he'll find a lonesome bird. "The old place" makes me wonder about days long ago.

The little road runs out, not really an abrupt end, it just sort-of "peters out," opening up into what's left of a field. I walk on, looking, searching, and see the old forest ahead. Off to the far right are two huge shrubs that bloom white in the spring. They are beautiful trees and from what I understand could have been imported. They seem to be the only ones, markers if you will, maybe even strategically planted. Hard to say with so many changes in a hundred and fifty years.

One time I just happened to be visiting with a grouse and woodcock guide who said, "Yeah, that place is quite grown up and the cover is getting old now, but it's usually good enough for a woodcock or two. Sometimes I do a quick hunt there."

Oh yes, now I remember; I bear hard right and then am about out of field. It's been quite some time since I've been here. Keep on walking, then a lot of tall grass, a large mound. I know it's here somewhere.

I see the large dark stone, lonely but grand in stature, right in the middle of nowhere and backed up against a forest of very mature evergreen trees. Without this looming stone, the rest of the little opening just becomes part of the landscape. Yes, it stands the tallest among more. There's a small concrete stone on the ground next to it marked WNW. This little place intrigues me! After some careful looking I find a boy, John, 1859, inscribed with "*A little time on earth he spent, Till God for him and his angels sent, And then on time he closed his eyes, To wake to glory in the skys* [age ten years]." Then a girl, Mary, died 1878, age twenty-two years. Old plastic flowers still there with Raleigh and Marjorie, from someone who cared, struggling to stay upright, with a place card holder, no card, it's certainly been there for some time.

Wandering back to the large stone sentinel, likened to a village watchman, I continue to poke around. The dog is usually content just keeping busy sniffing around the edges, checking in with me, wondering why I'm not coming. My back to the woods, I face the stone of a soldier, Hamlet, "*9th & 11th R.I. Vol. Inf., 3rd R.I. Vol. Cav.,*" a veteran of our great Civil War and his wife, Wilhelmina, "*Gone but not Forgotten.*" Stepping a bit to the right is a flat tablet covered heavily with moss and grass, the letters indiscernible until some careful scuffing from my shoe. There it is, Eliza D. Neal (1846–1906). Then there's a space, before an adjacent stone. Just ahead is a stone nearly tipped over. I straighten it; tuck some dirt behind to hold it straight. The space between just doesn't seem right, lots of heavy grass, a dry old dead limb laying there. I removed the limb, began pushing the grass aside and my suspicions are confirmed, another flat tablet, Joseph Neal (1816–1893), obviously, a husband and wife with thirty-years difference in age. I later learned there are fourteen residents of this nearly forgotten little village.

It was time to sit a moment, scratch my dog's ears and think. Probably it was a good chance for a smoke, not my preference, but a good spot for contemplation, nonetheless. The story about this place has gone with the ages, but I remember my father telling me he travelled by horse and wagon all morning with his dad to his grandfather's funeral here. We know it was not uncommon for farmers to have a small cemetery plot located on their land, a place for a family's final resting place. The sad thing is, unless someone remembers, someone who knew those folks, someone who cared, someone willing to mow, prune and maintain, any lasting human imprint may be lost forever amidst a regenerating forest.

Time to move on now, my Setter is waiting. I take a last look and cast "Max" toward a likely edge. Unless you remember where to look, that little road has blended into new growth, threatening to return the once cleared land to forest. We pass the two shrubs guarding that little corner. They surely were planted for a purpose. We often work that edge for a "spell" and when it runs out, cut back to the little road and head out. It's not a long hunt but always causes me to wonder what those folks did here, how they lived, how many children they had, and what brought them to this place. Bet there were a good many grouse here then.

You see, I have to check on "the old place" every year. Maybe there will be a bird for me, maybe not. No matter, maybe it's just an excuse. It may be the closest I ever get to hunt with my great-grandfather. Maybe that's really important!

Walking by the very last vestiges of the old foundation again and wondering what kind of house occupied this land was cause for a moment of reflection. Re-visiting that little cemetery and wondering about the folks resting there and the life they led posed many unanswered questions.

The next year I came early, before hunting season, the 29th of May, no gun, but armed with a shovel and a little box of ammunition…three geraniums; to keep a few lifetimes from fading into obscurity. You see, Hamlet and Wilhelmina Neal Wheaton were my great-grandparents; they built and owned that big house in the trees off Route 1 that I mentioned earlier, and here they rest on the corner of the old farm. Beside them are Joseph and Eliza Neal, my great-great-grandparents. They owned the house with the granite rock foundation that caught fire in the 1930s.

Leaving along the old edge, I turned for a quick look back and whispered to myself, "We'll be back, folks, maybe we'll find a bird next time… but, we'll be back!"

I'm sure you have visited an old homestead, a cellar hole filled with burdocks, old apple trees nearby, and found a few birds taking up residence, but then the wisdom of age, at times, recalls old dogs, old covers, and the sentiment of old times trumps a limit on birds. A few special old covers are just important for the soul.

Ken Berger connects on straight-away shot.

"Nathan" trying for cover.

Yard Bird

"Look, there's a bird, right there under that tree!" Ken said, matter of factly.

"Sure," I said, and lo and behold, just as I slow crawled the Suburban up the gravel driveway, a fine, gray grouse was grazing under a cedar tree just off the right side of the driveway, smack dab in the middle of camp. What possessed him to wander in from who knows where, just like a barnyard chicken, without a care in the world, is unexplainable.

Some "gray hairs" will remember the saga of "Walter," the elusive ten-pound rainbow trout that Norman Thayer called "a crafty old son-of-bitch" in the 1981 film *On Golden Pond*. Norman (Henry Fonda) and Billy Ray Jr. (Doug McKeon) fished for Walter until they finally caught him (then let him go), but the continued scheming and suspense to catch "Walter" made a good story.

"Walter" reminded me of this crafty old "yard bird."

Yours truly; our chef, Ken Berger; and Randy Havel, "The Great Morel" were taking a casual approach to the day one morning, a late start, so to speak. That Maine October morning with not a cloud in the sky, the sun warming slopes, just perfect to find a few birds filling their crops.

"Nathan," pecked along, gradually sauntering toward us, along the right-side edge of the gravel road, pondering a dash across the open country, then ducked his head making that mad dash in front of us. Now more comfortable with himself, he began to strut, only modestly alarmed, toward the tree lined hedgerow off to our left. Soon, when he had gained some distance between us, I suggested to Ken, "Let me turn off the engine, open your door very carefully, *leave it open*, then slip alongside to find your gun."

"This is surely going to be an exercise in futility," I said. "It usually is. But, let's just see if you can reach your gun. The bird will surely take off before you can load."

All those Chevrolet horses had been reined to a dead stop. The three of us had just sat there, burb quietly idling, watching "goober" peck away, strut and graze. Guns were all stowed in back near the dog crates. Bushwhacking, fairly common in this part of the world, was not our game, but once airborne, that's another matter. We were dumbfounded, engine still running, XM country music turned to silence.

The hedgerow consisted of a rock wall property line with a few bushes and some maturing maple and beech were approximately three-to-five inches wide. On the other side was the mowed lawn of the adjoining property, open for fifty yards to the next tree line. Old "Nathan," once he'd slipped into the narrow cover, was kerflummoxed and now faced a tough decision on just when to take wing, out across open ground, either way along the hedgerow edge, or simply back from where he came. I anticipated the bird's approaching dilemma.

"Hurry, he's in a box," I said to Ken. He managed to unzip his gun case, take the gun out, and drop two shells into his light Fox "A" grade 16 on a 20-gauge frame. Sneaking carefully, albeit uselessly with no cover above grass, the sneak consisted of quietly slipping across the lawn toward "Nathan."

By this time, both Randy and I had dismounted from the truck and fallen in behind Ken as he stalked his quarry, waiting for the bird to panic any second. No such luck! "Nathan" had ducked into the only possible cover, that hedgerow comprised of bushes, rocks, and trees, and began to march away to our left, dodging and darting between the stones, finding pathways through the little thickets.

"Ken," I said, "You better step right through that rock-filled boundary line and get on the other side, quickly." He did. The yard bird then was sort of between us. I caught glimpses of him bobbing and weaving, still marching to my left toward the lake, in quick step. He was well aware of his *pending precarious predicament.*

Interrupting the movie again, I spoke softly to Ken, "I am going around to his front in hopes the bird will flush back toward you." Remember, I'm on the open lawn and keeping my distance from the bird, trying not to spook him prematurely, while Randy is taking in the soap-box drama.

I succeeded in cutting off the ground escape route. Now I was just barely inside the edge of the hedgerow when the bird saw me and changed course, heading back from where it came, to my right. "Nathan" was keenly aware of the "roundup" underway. It was tough to find a pathway through the brush, but my challenge was to herd him toward Ken in a pincer move.

"He doesn't like it," I called out, "but, he's figured the game out, that it's safer on the ground than in the air," thinking to myself: *This bird is going to fly back from where he came, right over Randy's head and neither of us have guns. Ken will have no shot, just par for the course in grouse hunting.* Finally, I stepped out of the bushes, moved quickly up the hedge line and had "Nathan" jammed in a "box canyon." He goes left, then right, and is up against a sheer granite rock in front of him. A quick feint to my left, he dodges right, and I step into the tangle…now, I'm close. Finally, too much pressure and the bird flushes, *not* across the open field on either side of the hedgerow but tight to the little tree line, along the rock wall, straight toward the lake. Ken manages a quick straightaway shot and the rest is history.

Sure, you expected his escape, a plain old miss, but alas, his plan was foiled. That time our strategy worked. I can't vouch for this bird being the smartest, maybe he was a "village idiot," the gene pool won't miss him. The best laid plans seldom prove to work out, but in this rare instance our strategy was perfect. Grouse, or pa'tridge, again, as we say in New England, can be very clever, at times seemingly stupid, wary or tame, wily and wise, often all at the same time.

Hunting or really fishing for "Walter" was indeed the *real* thrill, decidedly more than the actual catch, the "the hunt or the stalk" to outwit old "Nathan" eclipsed the shot. The choice to shoot and release would provide the ultimate satisfaction, much like releasing Walter as "a gift to another sportsman."

New Brunswick, CA 2013
Fred Stump, Larry Frey, Randy Havel, Art Wheaton,
John Gaskins, Charles Stump with "Shay"

New Brunswick, CA 2014
Tim McKelvey, Larry Frey, Art Wheaton, Jim Baker, Fred Stump, Ken Berger

The Reverend Leroy and his Parker DHE 28 "fringed a pair"

Art and Minnesota grouse and woodcock expert biologist,
Earl Johnson at Pineridge Grouse Camp

Where Memories Are Made

Off a winding dirt road at the end of Drumming Log Lane lies a friendly oasis nestled among the pines. It's Pineridge Grouse Camp. From the time you arrive just before dusk in bird season, a quick survey noting cased double guns, bird dogs, SUVs, pick-up trucks, dog crates, dog dishes, orange vests, and hunters busy returning after a day in the field will confirm you are at the right place. Then, once inside, you will find the walls adorned with mounted grouse, old shotshell boxes, a rogue's gallery, and a floor gunrack against the wall with oar locks to rest the barrels. There's a den off the kitchen to sit and talk over the world's problems or the day's misses, with a TV, Internet connectivity, and a refreshment bar, if you so choose. This is where grouse talk, woodcock talk, dog talk, and gun talk permeate the walls, right under the sign of Gene Hill's great line, "Talk to me about the dogs, and the L. C. Smith, the Parker, the Lefever and the Ansley H. Fox." It's a special place where "memories are made."

One of the best spots in northern Minnesota specializing in grouse and woodcock is owned and operated by Randy and Jerry Havel. Good people! If you fly, you might get picked up in Bemidji in old "Buttercup," the restored 1953 GMC panel truck; if not, you'll be with a lot of other kindred spirits with your own SUV. Around camp you'll probably visit with guide and longtime biologist Earl Johnson from the Minnesota DNR who claims to know where there are a few good covers, catch third generation Parker Havel doing his many chores (especially cleaning birds), or listen to Randy and Jerry's stories. You'll be just as at home in camp as in the field.

I had the occasion to hunt a few hours with a couple of Virginians, Danny Morris and W. J. Worrell, the result of their kindly invite. About four hours later, "Dead-eye" Danny, with help from his Setter, "Clint," had dispatched four nice grouse, while W. J. and I just helped him swell his head. My shooting prowess proved wide of the mark.

Five Old Pats Society members came together once again to relive the good times, retell the old scams, tip one, and scare the hell out of a few birds. Randy, Chuck, Jerry and I had a 28-gauge Parker reunion one morning, firing volleys in a woodcock commune; some got away but some did not. His young Setter, "Rusty," was very busy with woodcock splash everywhere. Sometimes we had to crawl under an old log, testing a few rusty joints and stiff backs, but the action was wonderful. I don't remember the count, but it really didn't matter. Old friends together again confirmed it's not about the birds!

As we exited that cover a grouse quartered left right in front of me but in Randy's direction. He had a bad day from a full charge of my Remington Sporting Clays 8s. Randy kindly called out, "good shot," then, Jerry took a picture of us. That's the best part of it all, you know, the memory of our time together.

On another afternoon, Jerry blindfolded Chuck and I, put us in his truck, and stopped God knows where, alongside a cover on a sunny slope with snoozing grouse and couple of woodcock. Chuck did some damage, "fringing" two nice grouse with his Parker DHE 28. Jerry and I told him it was just luck or a golden "bb," but he insisted "fringing" was an art-form. Solid points from old "Gunner" were a highlight.

On the grub side, their walleye melts in your mouth. Pineridge serves up some woodcock poppers, hors d'oeuvres style, that will make the woodcock-shy change their minds about eating this bird. Meals like grouse breasts with capers and asparagus; or home-grown Angus ribeye, porterhouse, or bone-in-roast served family style will make you sleep well. Of course, you might want to chill out with a cigar and a little guitar strumming around the fire-pit…it might trip your trigger. The cook, Kevin Burt, tried some "blues" on us till we coached him into "Willie." One evening, writer "Tread Slough" picked some guitar on a little "Merle," "Waylon," and "Johnny," but singing around the table wasn't top-hit caliber. One could debate whether the before-dinner social exchanges—enhanced with ice cold beer on tap, maybe a smooth Tennessee whisky, or an aged single malt—or a few songs from Kevin please you the most, you are deep in Grouse Country.

At Pineridge, you will be one of the gang. No Hilton bus boys, this is the real deal! We talk about our guns, show our guns, tell stories, brag about dogs, eat good, sleep well, and hope it never ends. I know, because Randy and I have been good friends for forty-plus years, Jerry from when Halloween pumpkins were important to him, and now with Parker we're all Old Pats Society members. If you want to be around the heart and soul of grouse and woodcock gunning, this is it, but plan well in advance.

Charles Stump, Fred Stump, & Jerry Havel at Pineridge Grouse Camp

Charles Stump, first grouse; New Brunswick, Canada

Take the Shot

His words rang out loud and clear, "I wasn't ready." *Duh*! A friend of mine yelled out, "What do you want him to do, mail you a letter?"

Expletives, some even poetic, describing an escaping grouse are endless. Some of those choice words are not publishable, but you have heard the many excuses. Even with a limited mental capacity and years at this game, except for the odd grouse that flew into my screened-in porch or hit the glass dining room window and fell dead, never has one been brought to bag without firing a shot.

One late afternoon many years ago, hunting grouse in Connecticut with some friends, we were working the thickest section of a fish and game club property when a grouse flushed wild just in front of me. I glimpsed it for a brief instant as it disappeared into the heavy leaves about fifteen feet off the ground. The old Parker 20 Trojan quickly came to the shoulder and barked after pulling the front trigger. The remaining sight picture was only the spot where he disappeared. It happened so fast, the gun mount, pulling the front trigger and leaves falling from the impact of the shot string that I don't even remember seeing the bird when the gun went off. A miss, for sure!

"Didja get 'em?" Ken hollered to me.

"Don't think so," I replied, then decided to investigate the general area of the shot but with little or no confidence of success. It was more a courtesy to the bird than myself, but it deserved a look. There was no sound, thud, or wing beat in the fallen leaves; in fact, there was no discernable hint of contact. As I slipped though the brush where the bird escaped, parting the whips and heavy leaf cover, it opened up just a bit beyond where the shot was taken. Once through, the ground was bare and confirmed my suspicion of a yet another miss. As I opened the gun and looked where the shot had cleared out some leaves, my eyes focused on the crotch of a small maple and there, stuck as if placed with his neck in the *Y* was a fine grouse, stone dead.

B.S. luck? Good shooting? Beats me! This was a prime example of "taking the shot."

Another time I glimpsed a crosser, just a flash, mind you, the result of a friend calling, "Mark" on a bird flush that was not visible to me or within hearing. With the gun at the ready, it was a classic poke and shoot, relying on senses learned from years of gunning. The bird was in sight for only an instant, then it disappeared through a mass of leaves and brush. There was only a moment to mount the gun, establish a sight picture, and pull the trigger. The obligatory search began by crawling through the dense thicket of tangles, thorns, and briars. That once-smart old biddy lay folded on a bed of aspen and maple leaves. The bird simply had that bad hair day. Call it instinctive shooting or luck again. Probably more of the latter for me!

No need to preach to the choir of seasoned grouse and woodcock hunters. This is not a game to *save* ammunition and certainly not one to wait for a *good clear shot*. Rarely does that happen!

Charles C. Norris in his *Eastern Upland Shooting* (copyright 1946) writes: "...shoot if necessary at the flash of a wing where he thinks the bird ought to be, it is surprising how often the dog will bring in the bird." And he goes on: "The thing to do is to make up your mind that you will not wait for a clear definition, but fire instantly; you cannot be too quick in firing in what appears to be the line of flight taken by the bird. Even in cover so thick that it is almost impossible to get through, such shots can frequently be brought off." Should you think for one minute this game is easy, forget it, but it is that great challenge that keeps us coming back.

For those who are new at the game, excited about chasing the king, a solid piece of good advice is to make the best of any opportunity. When the whirr of wings, a sudden upward flush, a quick crosser, or just a flash in a narrow opening in the brush occurs, it may be all you get. Norris's sage advice is simple: "When grouse shooting, there is no time to pick shots and count cartridges."

Most of the time a hurried shot leaves one dumbfounded with an open chamber, an ejected shell, and no contact. The unexpected flush always seems to scare the hell out of you, but regaining a presence of mind to get off another shot with calculated smoothness and confidence often brings a bird to bag. Take advantage of even the slimmest of opportunities.

The attraction to ruffed grouse hunting is linked directly to the level of difficulty. Each bird is a trophy, each shot and every flush exciting, and each trip afield banks another rich adventure. The excitement you experience from the deafening split second of silence, instantly interrupted by the beating of wings in the leaves identifying your downed bird, or the surprise when your dog returns with a bird in his mouth will be convincing evidence that playing the hand you are dealt sometimes makes you a winner.

We never seem to get weary of taking a fine ruffed grouse on the wing. It still excites me after fifty years. If it didn't, I'd quit. When a newcomer shoots his first grouse, we all are pleased, as we know he will be back for more.

Take the shot, it's the one reason we do what we do! Missing is part of it all and some of the greatest misses provide the best laughs, but our first is never forgotten.

Art Wheaton—"cold as hell"

Rick Robison, Vic Romano, Scott Hanes, Art Wheaton, Ken Berger
on Upper Peninsula, Michigan

Minefields in Michigan

"I'm getting a little worried about the dogs," Ken piped up. Normally "Lucy," my English Setter; "Pax" and "Brandy," Ken's English Setter and Brittany, nestled in their sky kennels in the back of the Suburban and station wagon, had plenty of protection. But we were becoming concerned as the thermometer moved toward sub-zero. In the short time we had been there, the temperature slid steadily downward; radio reports warned it would go even lower. "As long as we have plenty of wood for the fire," we thought, "we will be fine."

"I'll take the single bed," Vic quickly volunteered, thinking the spot nearest the fire would be the warmest.

"Okay," I responded, "the top bunk down the hall will work out just fine for me." Scott, Ken, and Rick found bunk beds adjacent to the bathroom. One last trip outside to restore personal comfort was essential.

Ken, bothered by the weather, made up his mind and said, "I'm going to bring my dogs in."

"That's a really good plan," I agreed.

The treat of such deluxe accommodations, close to the roaring fire, might be a bit extravagant for some hunting dogs but their well-being was our first priority. A straw and insulated enclosure was normally the comfortable and familiar home for Ken's kenneled dogs. Now their new cabin surroundings made them restless and uncertain of proper sleeping arrangements. "The hatches were battened down" so to speak as we stoked the fire one last time. Occasional pitter patter of toenails on the linoleum signaled the dogs kept searching for just the right spot to curl up. One or two made an attempt to climb on someone's bunk but were turned away with a stern order or a brush of the hand.

We had arrived in Gulliver, Michigan, just ahead of a surprise cold front. Frigid Arctic air was moving quickly across the northern tier, with full force due later that night. How cold could it get? Our hardy crew, well acquainted with cool fall weather, was ready to hunt in spite of such adversity. The grouse wouldn't care—neither should we.

That fall, members of the Old Pats Society had struggled to find time between pressing business schedules for our annual hunt. Every proposed date ran into a snag. As the weeks and months dragged into summer, dates once thought good got cancelled. New obligations appeared. It became increasingly apparent that if an Old Pats hunt materialized at all, it would be a skeleton crew. Finally, a November date was set, this time to the Upper Peninsula of Michigan where the "Yoopers" hang out. We weren't really "trolls," those past the bridge in lower Michigan, maybe just out-of-staters invading this new country for its storied reputation for grouse and woodcock.

Ken Berger and Rick Robison were to meet us at resort cabins in Gulliver on Wednesday night, fully loaded with dogs and gear in Ken's Suburban. They would motor through Ohio and Lower Michigan to meet Messer's Romano, Wheaton, and Hanes. Wheaton would pick up Romano and Hanes at the Escanaba airport, then proceed to "camp." albeit not without a good laugh at a restaurant/bar along the way.

A bit road weary with the thought of a good cocktail and bite to eat, they took a pit stop. The waitress said, "Can I get you a drink?"

Ken replied, "I'll have a 'Stoly' on the rocks."

Rick chimed in with, "Make mine a double of the same."

She returned shortly and asked, "What is a 'Stoly'?" Ken responded that Stolichnaya is a Russian vodka and away she went, soon to return saying, "We don't have 'Stoly,' but we have 'Popov.'"

"OK," they said with a little chuckle under their breath, realizing the tariff was a bit steep for high dollar alcoholic beverages in this rural area.

Libations secured, we eventually found our oasis deep in grouse country. The welcoming party met us with flashlights in hand, Ken quickly announcing, "The temperature is supposed to drop severely." But after a wee dram of Scotch, some raucous laughter from telling great old stories amidst the smell hanging over a blazing wood fire of seasoned hardwood, our spirits were lifted, dreaming of thundering birds and a new flight of woodcock. With a little grub and roughly laid plans for the morrow, we decided to turn in. All the while, the chilling wind took temperatures lower by the hour.

Five a.m. came fast. The fire had long gone out. Frigid air penetrated our sleeping quarters. I hollered out, "Hey, somebody stoke up that fire!" No reply.

Then somebody softly laughed and announced, "Dogs need to go out."

"Yeah, yeah," I said, "Go for it."

Wrestling with the covers, tossing around to find a tight sleeping bag wrap for the best comfort, and fighting a growing urge brought on by an overfilled bladder, I could stand it no longer. Relieving myself of this pain resulted in a pioneering effort to find the facility in complete darkness. But first, the noise of three dogs, prancing and dancing, needed attention. I gave in, pulled back the covers and planted my bare feet solidly on the cold cabin floor where two senses of urgency collided. Something had to give. The dogs won out. In the kitchen, a circus act was in progress.

I felt my way through the bedroom doorway into the hall. My companions remained motionless, either sound asleep or faking it. I had drawn the short straw and was tasked with letting the dogs out, not by assignment, but by my own inability to put up with the pandemonium, often surpassed by the growing discomfort between my legs.

Gingerly navigating toward the noise in the kitchen, guided by the mere hint of light coming through the window, I entered the circus tent and headed for the front door. Then, *squish*. One bare foot set down in a soft mound that oozed between my toes.

"Damn," I said to myself, then offered out loud, "Oh, crap!" even louder. "This place is a minefield!" I yelled into the black room, then shifted my weight to the heel of one foot while I hobbled forward to bring the other foot down in another moist pile.

These terrible-smelling land mines were mixed with cellophane wrappers, napkins, and other bits of paper debris. With another step, my voice hit another octave, much louder this time: "OH CRAP!"

There was another minefield of dog patties, and no matter how careful my negotiation, each step landed in one of them. Now half way to the door, hobbling on both heels, with dogs running in circles, I managed to increase my pace, sideswipe another landmine, and open the door, only to be nearly swept away by the bumping and pushing of dogs trying to get through the narrow doorway all at the same time. Seemingly stranded there for the moment, reality set in when the frigid air hit me in the face. I slammed the door and beat a hobbling, hasty retreat toward the bathroom in hopes of immediate relief from the clinging mushy remains of dog deposits in between my toes and under my ankles.

The velocity of both animated and vocal condemnation of my plight, accompanied by a number of colorful four-letter expletives, caused my comrades to stir and chuckle. With the bathroom located, relief was at hand, expected from a good dose of warm running water. Throwing one foot over the edge of the sink, I leaned forward to turn on the faucets. Nothing. With both taps turned all the way open—not a drip.

"Damn it, the water's froze up," I called out. "Plumbing is frozen tight."

Now I was stranded while my Old Pats comrades lay relishing the spectacle from the comfort of their bunks, their imaginations gone wild over my predicament. Not one expressed a hint of sympathy.

Maneuvering again on my heels around the sink, I grabbed a roll of paper towels; that offered some relief. All towels became fair game. What could a good man do? Appearing trapped, I had to make the best of a lousy predicament. Experiencing a modicum of relief from the globs of clinging dog patties, the work of removal continued while the pungent smell lingered.

Negotiating my way back to the bedroom, past the kitchen, was precarious. Now to get warm. No turning back: get quickly to my clothes in the bedroom utilizing what little daylight was gathering in the windows. Slipping on my pants while trying to avoid touching parts of my feet was a challenge. The real test was to put on my shoes. Shall I go for the socks first or skip them?

Finally, I gave up. I put on the socks and shoes because there was no hope for water, then headed outside to complete one of the original missions.

Once again slipping through the minefield, the cause of the chaos became apparent. Strewed hither and yon were bread bags. Then it hit me: the dogs had eaten all eight loaves of bread and rolls on the kitchen counter. The ruckus resulted from competition to see who could eat the most, the fastest. Our bread was all gone. I don't know which dog got the best of it, but the gigantic mess—bread bags ripped to pieces and patties aplenty—would have been enough for a divorce in any man's home. It's a good thing this was a rental cabin. Back home we all would have been sent packing.

The guys commenced to stir, then icy reality set in: it was just too damn cold to stay there.

Stupidity was not our strong suit. The Old Pats beat a hasty retreat to the local Ramada Inn. Memories of the birds flushed and shot on that trip have faded, but my little dance on the linoleum is as clear as if it had been shot in high-def. Yeah, and who could ever forget the smell.

Dad's shotshell bag and compass

Dear old "Rags"

Shell Bag Memories

He kept the old shell bag on the top shelf of the hall closet.

That magical old bag sat nestled amongst his hunting stuff in a very narrow closet space—maybe a couple of feet wide—without a door. A thin curtain hung from a closet rod and covered the lower shelves of linen. The rod had to be removed to get to the top shelf. On that one little hidden shelf, beyond my reach, Dad also stored his old H&R Model 999 revolver in a hand-made leather holster, a couple of dog-eared boxes of paper Remington and Peters shotgun shells, a box of Kleanbore rifle cartridges, his hunting knife, and a compass.

In those days, country folks didn't have a gun cabinet to show or store their guns. Most owned only one gun or two: a 12-gauge shotgun and a deer rifle which stood in a corner or behind a door. Dad had an old Lefever 12-gauge Nitro Special and a Remington Model 14 in .32 Remington Special. But it was that musty, smoky-smelling shotgun shell bag with its draw string closure that held the real treasure, the never-forgotten memories.

Dad told me about his family's first bird dog, "Rags," "a mongrel Fox Spaniel of sorts," he said. "He was a treeing dog. He'd bark, he'd tree them, and we'd go shoot them. Lots of nights I'd go with that dog after school and get five or six birds. The first year we used him I shot sixty birds." The story came alive when I found the snapshot of "Dear Old Rags" while leafing through a long-forgotten photo album.

I eventually summoned enough courage to ask if he would let me find a pat'ridge of my own.

After serving the ultimatum, "You must go alone," we went to the special closet. Dad reached up, slid the curtain to one side and took down the red plaid shell bag, opened the draw string, felt around and handed me four shells. The images of those casings stay etched in my mind. Some were Remington Express Kleanbore, others Peters High Velocity in sizes 5, 6 and 7½. The high-brass green ribbed cases were stamped lengthwise on the case and the brass had Remington UMC imprinted near the top, their crimps sealed with a sticker marked 3¾–1¼–7½. The Peters were blue, smooth-sided paper, also with a top sticker, marked CHILLED SHOT. Forever CHILLED SHOT stuck as my recipe for success, even though the term is not a part of today's ammunition. This to me as a young gunner was a prized medicine bag with its own magic.

The old woods road up to Daugherty ridge behind our house was my first grouse covert. If you picked your way carefully along the trail, avoiding pockets of fallen leaves, choosing the more barren spots to step, maybe using a few exposed moss-covered rocks or bare piece of ledge, you might sneak within range of an old biddy. The stalking technique was to stop, look, and listen; sneak a few more steps; and then do it all over again, trying to identify a pa'tridge scratching along with beech nuts on her mind. The charge of 7½s from the old bag found a target that fall afternoon, and when I showed up at the back door with that trophy bird. It was a proud moment but forever his words served as one of life's lasting lessons.

There was something extraordinary about that old shell bag. It was likened to a treasure chest packed with coins. Each shell held the key to adventure, ready for another hunting trip. Every shell was treated with utmost care and held the potential to bag a pat'ridge, duck, rabbit, or squirrel. At the local Pine Tree Store, in those days you could purchase shotgun shells one at a time, take groceries on credit, and find Half and Half chewing tobacco if you were so inclined. The shells cost a dime. Our hunting satisfaction was defined by what was brought to bag, not flush counts as today. It was country culture not to waste shells by blasting at flushed birds; there was no money to waste.

Dad got us a bird dog, an English Setter that Mother named "Spot." She had private quarters, right on the floor behind the wood-burning cookstove. She became a great pal. My father hunted with her but we lost her early, never having the chance to take her up the trail. Dogs care about you; I learned a lot from "Spot," and my affection was returned, resulting in my being hooked on Setters forever.

That soft red plaid treasure chest made me feel like Captain Kidd with an illusion of richness. Dipping my hand in the opened bag, extracting a handful of shells, they could have been gold pieces. Shotgun shells were hard to come by and wild game helped a strained food budget.

The pouch had a red corduroy bottom that attached to a plaid top with brass buttons in slotted or elongated button holes about 1½ inches from the bottom. Maybe in some ways it felt like a western-style bandolier but was never carried across the shoulder. The top, with its draw string, could be removed by unbuttoning it from the brass buttons. It was the nicest shell bag I've ever known.

The old shell bag came with us each time Dad took me duck hunting. Often, he would say, late in the afternoon, "Let's see if we can find a duck," and would take me in the Grand Laker canoe to the headwaters of a small stream where ducks settled in toward dusk. That bag would be on the floor at his feet so he could quickly grab a couple of shells. Sometimes he would position me on the bank, sneak into the woods, to appear at just the right place, jumping the ducks to fly over me. I lost my wallet on one such trip; it probably fell in the grass or water, never to be found again, but other than a boy's loss of a few dollars, the loss faded, while memories of the trip remained.

That neat old shell bag has moved with me to each new home, sometimes it stayed in a box, in a closet, behind the framed glass door of my maple gun cabinet, or on the shelf in a gun safe, but it has gracefully aged, growing in importance as it sat perched on the mantel of my den, where each day it speaks to me in a barely discernable whisper, like a soft gentle breeze, here and gone, "Remember the time." There seems to be a bit of

Dad's spirit resting inside, the imprint of his hands and fingers around those drawstrings, his fingerprints on those old green ribbed Remington and the smooth blue Peters shells, and a faint ghost-like image (or maybe it's just in my mind) of him dropping two of those duck loads in the barrels of that 12-gauge Lefever Nitro Special. From its perch, each day it overlooks the goings on in my gun room den-office and watches me wipe down a fine Parker gun, tie a bass bug leader, or craft some words in hopes another sportsman can find a moment of solace in the stories that collectively enrich a sporting life. It has an invaluable measure of comfort.

Dad is gone, but most certainly his soul lives with the old shell bag. Now it's mine, a cherished reminder of the past. It looks and smells the same. At times, it brings a salty tear from flashed scenes of seasons long past. That old bag and the "potion" locked therein mean a lot to me.

Once a friend asked me, "How come you keep that old ladies' purse?" but he could not break the spell from life's precious memories. What the hell does he know about shell bags?

Old Pats Society 2012—Forest City, ME
(rear left to right) Allan Swanson, Roger Lowell, Randy Havel, Ken Waite Jr., Ken Waite III,
Matt Ambrose, Tim McCormack, Jon Foster, Art Wheaton, Jim Ryan, Chuck Mosher,
(front) Charles Stump, Fred Stump

Silver Setter at Pineridge Grouse Camp

Chuck & Randy at Pineridge Grouse Camp:
"Take that, Jim. The six months ran out."

Jim with a replacement Silver Setter and
an English pointer, at the Baltimore
Gun Show: "Take this, Chuck and
Randy, I found a replacement."

The Silver Setter

The dusty, seemingly ancient black Setter had been "locked" on a perfect point, barely discernible atop the table among an array of knick-knacks and scarcity antiques. This kidnapped, classic bird dog, poised in a style painted by artists at the turn of the century, appeared to an occasional passerby as just timeworn porcelain, tired and scuffed with age. Folks would not give even the slightest glance at an undistinguished dog with tail slightly separated from his body amidst the rest of the clutter offered for sale. The dealer really had no sense of value, just that it was old, dirty, *folksy*, and in poor condition.

The scene unfolded at the Brimfield, Massachusetts, antique show, one of if not the largest in the country, where the old dog just held his point, the best he could muster beneath amateurishly applied black paint, now chipped in places so only a trained eye could detect the tiniest glint of silver visible through a scar or scuff. Then one day a discriminating sporting gentleman, Dr. Kenneth Waite Jr., whose observant eyes spied him, envisioned a special quality buried beneath that, if exposed, might liven the intensity and class of this fine dog. With some trepidation, he reached deep in his normally tight pocket and extracted sufficient greenbacks to bring him home, following his own sage advice as a guide, "When you see it and it's right, buy it." Now, the old Setter would have a rightful home among other sporting collectables, to be properly displayed for admiring and appreciative sportsman.

What most casual observers would not have noticed is that this chiseled pose is likened to greatness, reminiscent of the classic paintings of Edmund H. Osthaus. This premier artist is known for capturing that famous style so represented in this Setter—intensity, straight tail, and lifted front leg are indicative of the renowned artist's works.

The old scrounger himself, the Good Doctor knew that these figurines were sold through jewelry stores, and sometimes an English Pointer and rarely a Springer Spaniel were cast by the same maker. The professional castings were done in seven pieces, then soldered together. Grouse and woodcock hunters who have a keen sense of the rich history surrounding good Setter dogs find the style attractive and representative of a golden age.

Dr. Waite rushed home, anxious to see if his instincts would prove correct. He immediately attempted removal of the poorly applied, black finish. Retired to the confines of his basement "man cave," the Good Doctor first carefully dabbed a little bit of paint stripping gel to the belly section. From this rather obscure spot underneath, beautiful silver materialized. An hour later, the previously disguised "Silver Setter," AKA "Silver," emerged in brilliant form with all his glory, newly dressed for an honored spot on the physician's desk among other prized collectables: an English Pointer of that same maker and the 1935 National Sportsman Trophy from Cleveland, Ohio, donated by *National Sportsman Magazine*, William Harnden Foster, editor, for "High-Over-All Winner" at this first-ever National Skeet Shoot.

The weeks ticked by, then one evening at 8p.m. his cell phone rang. "Hello Jim," the Good Doctor said, his attention then diverted from a local town meeting in progress.

James Jay Baker recognizing immediately that his friend was busy, asked, "What have you got for me?" (The occasion was only a few days prior to the upcoming 2013 Maryland Arms Collectors Show, AKA, the Baltimore Gun Show.)

"Well" the Doctor responded, "I'll take a look." Arriving at the Hunt Valley Inn for the scheduled kick-off luncheon, Dr. Waite came to the table and he and Jim quickly disappeared to the trunk of his car. "Silver" appeared under the lid of a cardboard box, red tag priced at $550. After a short negotiation, "Silver" was reduced to $400. "I'll take it," responded Jim, with only a modest inspection.

So, you ask, what's all the fuss over a beat-up, grungy old black and now Silver Setter statue with a broken tail? Well, perhaps you need to be a seasoned grouse and woodcock hunter, an English Setter bird-dog man, have read some of the early Setter glory days of the Grand National Championship to truly appreciate him. Recall great Setters like "Count Gladstone IV," "Count Noble," "Lady's Count Gladstone," "Tony's Gale" or even reflect on the image of Gleam's "Gladstone Max," pictured in the August 1929 issue of *Hunting and Fishing* to relish the "throw-back" of old "Silver." "Silver's" horizontal tail, rather than the high, nearly straight-up style of today and his crouched intensity, often portrayed in the paintings of Edmund Osthaus and G. Muss Arnolt, make this turn-of-the-century Setter image immortal in the minds of dog men.

Jerry Robinson, the wonderful and talented writer from his piece in *Sports Afield*, February 1975 characterized the Setter best, (paraphrasing):

> It's been said that Setter men share a deeper bond of understanding with their dogs, that the Setter has a way of wending its way into the heart of every member of a family and some say Setter men are odd, they talk to their dogs. The reassuring thump of his tail and the way he looks at you is validation that he has a remarkable understanding for human vocabulary.

And quoting directly:

> You don't just shoot with a setter, you share profound moments with him. It's not unlikely for you to even have a drink with him on more occasions than owners of other breeds would ever understand. The

English setter can make your skin crawl with sensations of pleasure and reward you with a vision of beauty and grace that warms you long after the memory of the moment dims.

So it is we Setter folks reflect on those special days with dogs like "Silver." He will take us to abandoned apple orchards, alder runs, frosty mornings, and sunny hillsides for the flush of a grouse or woodcock.

That Saturday in Baltimore, while "Silver" stayed patiently on point amongst high-quality English Greener shotguns, Parker hammer guns, and a fine Huey oak case, the "buzzards" began circling. A cast of admirers including Chuck Mosher, AKA, the Reverend Leroy, and Randy Havel, AKA, the Great Morel, began the swooping, pecking, and prancing as they zeroed in on this great Setter. Another deal was incubating!

The said "deal" finally agreed to by all parties present was consummated as follows: in exchange for a very small (many would say inadequate) check in the amount of $450, Purchaser (Havel) agrees with the now Seller (Baker) to the following terms and conditions regarding the transfer of said Setter (AKA "Silver"): "Silver" will be repaired, cared for by Havel for six months, and thereafter transferred to the Reverend Leroy for the following six months, said transfer to occur every six months hereafter, unless and until said Havel is deceased, at which time "Silver" reverts to rightful owner Baker (the self-proclaimed aggrieved party and seller with $50 to the good).

Hence old "Silver" came into my possession, albeit briefly, for the careful packing and shipment fees prior to his Minnesota journey, where he has now undergone expert solder repair and restoration.

He now proudly looks on from a vantage look-out high on a shelf at Pineridge Grouse Camp, next to his likeness painted by Edmund Osthaus. There he can listen to Earl Johnson pontificate whether a woodcock was left-handed or not, hear Randy extol the virtues of Parker-dom, and occasionally curl his lip when libation has loosened the lips of an Old Pats Society member who embellishes the truth.

So, what is the point, you say? Well, "Silver" is a symbol of good times, of dear old friends, of the adventures that made our lives so much richer, and of the heightened upland shooting experience. Sportsman will surround themselves with meaningful stuff, be it Dad's old shell bag, a mahogany cleaning rod, briar-worn deerskin gloves, "Lucy's" collar, an Elmer Crowell decoy, fired shells from that double…all of which define us; it is who we are, and we are proud of it.

Parker's Parker, 2008

Jerry Havel, Parker Havel, Randy Havel with Parker VH 20

Gun Show Surprise

William Parsons (1855–1932)

"May Heaven Reward Him with a Parker,
A Good Dog, and Plenty of Partridge"

It was a defining moment!

"Oh no, you forgot to pack it?" fourteen-year-old Parker said. He had counted on Randy, his granddad, to ship his Fox gun to Maine for the Old Pats Society hunt. Bitter disappointment was written all over his face.

This story really began in "Steel Town" long ago when a Parker gun showed up unsuspectingly in a furniture deal. It was a love affair at first sight, everlasting, passionate, and enduring, then cradled, carried, cleaned, and cared for like a child for over forty years. She killed many a grouse and woodcock before her master crossed over the great divide. Then one day, a perfect surprise occurred when the gun landed in the arms of a new and budding Old Pats Society member, to live the old times once again.

Once in a while, there's a wonderful little story that warms the heart.

When a gun with special provenance finds a new home, the right home for a lifelong partnership with a third-generation gunner, a memory is created that lasts forever.

This is that story.

Over forty-five years ago, I made friends with some folks on the clay target circuit around Steel Town. In those days (1969–1972), Pittsburgh was bustling with gun clubs that circled the city. West Penn, Millvale, North Side, Clairton, and Ruffsdale Gun clubs, to name a few, were thriving with league and registered shooting. Every weekend there was a registered event, and any weeknight one could shoot-practice.

One day after breaking targets, I kibitzed with John and Marie Wray over our mutual interest in Parker guns. Neither John nor I could afford what we would like but had been smitten by "Old Reliable." Then our lives went in different directions. However, I always remembered John and his love of grouse hunting and Parker guns.

Fast forward to 2007, a surprise recorded telephone message appeared from Marie. I returned the call, saddened to learn that John had passed away in July and Marie was worried about his Parker guns, wondering who she might trust to sell them.

She told me, "I was praying John would give me a signal on what to do and I began flipping through old issues of *Parker Pages*, found your name, and made the call."

Needless to say, it was a bittersweet reunion. This very nice but sad lady, filled with emotion and a sense of loss on her hands, talked about John, his love of Parkers through his life, and now what should she do? It was a difficult time for her. She asked me to help her with John's Parkers.

John had said, "These guns are a little *nest egg* for you after I'm gone," but he had never explained to her how and where to sell them.

Over the next few months, I helped her find new homes for his guns at fair market prices with all proceeds going to her. However, in the process, old no 155,XXX "spoke to me."

The character of this gun; with hang tag, its honest wear, smooth checkering, silver receiver, and untouched screws; in what I deemed "used but never abused" condition, struck me as one that should not go the way of a gun show table. It deserved better! It was John's personal grouse gun. I finally just bought it myself to preserve it for such a time when someone might surface that deserved to be its steward for another generation.

In a little packet with the gun I discovered a 3x5-lined-card bill of sale reflecting its purchase by John on 5/4/64, and with it a white-lined half sheet of tablet paper with the results of a shooting test at forty yards with 2½" shells, showing that the chokes were IC & Mod.

I wanted to learn more. It prompted me to call Marie again. She told me that she and John had gone to the home of a Mr. Arthur P. Ives to purchase a dining room set they needed badly. The set was available for $200, so the deal was consummated…a lot of money for a carpenter.

Somehow the conversation turned to guns, as Mr. Ives was a miniature pistol collector of sorts. A bit of show and tell followed and almost by divine intervention, old 155,XXX came out of the closet.

John asked the price and was quoted $150; however, *all* his money had been spent on the furniture. The story goes that John had to borrow the money from his mother to own this, his very first Parker, which became his prized grouse gun that he would carry for over forty years.

Its long and varied tour of duty found it in the covers of Mercer and Crawford counties of Pennsylvania, in Michigan, Minnesota, and Ohio. Like many avid grouse and woodcock hunters, John also had a vast library of grouse and woodcock books, including a complete set of the *Double Gun Journal* and *Parker Pages*. He also loved his English Setters, "Duke," "Ruffie," and "Dawn" of the DeCoverly-Ryman lines. Marie commented that John spent hours cleaning, oiling, and polishing his treasured possession.

I reflected for weeks on this new information, all of which supported my original assessment that this gun was special. Then a thought jumped into my mind that my good friend and Old Pats Society founder, "The Great Morel," Randy Havel, was scheduled to bring his son, Jerry, and grandson, Parker, to our annual hunt in Maine. A little electronic transmission to him with a condensed version of the story of this gun, its provenance, and my thoughts for a new owner yielded an exciting positive response. Then I fired back to him with a more complete story and how the new owner needed to give it the lifelong care it deserved, along with continued exposure to the brambles, briers, alder runs, and apple tree coverts across the country. A plan was hatched whereby it would indeed find a new home at the Old Pats Society hunt in October.

Then I decided to go the extra mile, to find out what was listed on her birth certificate. It appears this Parker was originally ordered by a Mr. Johnson of Pittsburgh, Pennsylvania, as the original Parker order book records call out a Parker VH 20 with 26" or 28" barrels with a weight of 6 lbs. 2oz. Stock dimensions were requested at 2⅞" or 3" drop at heel. This gun was manufactured December 28, 1911. It was ordered and shipped to Mr. J. A. Johnson, ultimately with 26" barrels, 1⅝" drop at the comb and 2⅞" drop at the heel. It had the usual standard double triggers, splinter forend, dog's-head butt plate, and pistol-grip cap, as it did the day it was shipped. The character of this fine gun speaks of good solid use and care, with its worn, nearly smooth checkering, silver receiver, silver forend iron, and tang. Case color exists just north of the trigger guard, on the water table and on the barrel side of the forend iron, very typical of its age and use.

It was a good choice for a grouse and woodcock gun with IC & Mod chokes. The gap in its life span, we will likely never fill; nor will we know when Mr. Johnson parted with the gun or who might have owned it until it landed in Mr. Arthur P. Ives's collection.

As with most guns, any recorded history of its owners and use have long disappeared, but the fifty-three years before it found a new home with John Wray, it likely stayed in the Pittsburgh area. But that story does not end now. Its new home, maybe for the next fifty years, is *the rest of the story*.

The plan was consummated by Randy to surprise his grandson on "gun show night," Tuesday, October 28, 2008. Spirits were high as Randy, the Great Morel, and his son, Jerry, awaited the time for our adult version of "bring and brag." The traditional arrival dinner for Old Pats members with brats on the grill and good libation was soon followed by the "Gun Show," a collection of great double guns.

Old 155 was dressed in a special-fitted leather trunk case containing all the pictures, hang tag, notes, letter from the Parker Gun Collectors Association and with a defining letter to Parker Havel that captured, chronologically, the history of this gun, beside a *personal* letter from Randy to his grandson.

That evening guns were "hefted" and pointed at imaginary grouse on the wall, forends and barrels removed, marks and condition inspected. "The Good Doctor," Ken Waite Jr., pointed to a cased gun and turned it over to find a taped letter addressed to Parker Havel on the reverse side.

He announced, "Hey, Parker, this must be yours."

Parker responded, "No, I don't have a gun here."

Ken followed, "Well, it's got your name on it, so you perhaps might check it out."

The room exploded with camera flashes. He took the gun from its case, assembled it with great care, now speechless, yet beaming with excitement and grinning from ear-to-ear.

The moment had arrived! He took the letter, opened it and began to read. With all eyes fixed on a lifetime event for this young man, his dad and granddad could not have been prouder and Parker could not have been happier. The next day, he was officially indoctrinated into the Old Pats Society by biting the head from a grouse, then awarded the Old Pats Society pin and cap.

Parker went on to shoot his limit of woodcock twice during the week. The grin never left his face. He reread all the papers that accompanied this gun, even learned some new language reserved for use later in life. His cell phone seemed always lit up as he could not stop talking to his mom about the gun, the trip, the great time, and his gun show surprise.

Watercolor, "The House Outback" by author's mother, Ruth E. Wheaton

The House Outback

Some come here to sit and think, others to…a familiar line.

The reading library for many old hunting camps is usually piled in a stack, surviving frigid, hot and humid, mosquito and black fly weather, off by itself, where kings make a daily visit to this kingdom, perch on the throne of contemplation and become master of their domain. This special place, where one can quietly read, think, muse, reflect, and remember is a regular depository of used culinary delights. As important as the pot-bellied heater stove, each grand old hunting camp had a "House Outback" designed to restore personal comfort. From the little-known booklet titled *The Grouse Hunters* their destination was called "Little Egypt."

It seemed the rightful final resting place for the outdated Sears & Roebuck or Montgomery Ward catalogs, where prices remain constant but those broad offerings are gradually reduced page by page with each thoughtful session. This is also the place where it is taboo to rip pages from faded and prized sporting magazines: a 1935 *Outdoor Life*, a 1940 *Field & Stream* or a *National Sportsman* with maybe a William Harnden Foster, Hy Watson, or Arthur Fuller cover and within, great stories on grouse shooting and adventures in the North Woods that are still good reading today.

In today's fast-paced world, it's tough to find time to just think. Camp can provide a great opportunity to commiserate with your inner thoughts, better focus on things you want to do, reflect on missions completed, or just to have some quiet moments to strategize about the future and take care of immediate business, the final event, if you will, in preparation for a great gunning day ahead.

When the leaves burst into their most vivid colors, then are interrupted by a killing frost that signals the beginning of their descent, sportsman all across this great country head for a rustic and remote camp to be "away from it all," to chase the wily buck, bruin, or once again visit those ruffed grouse coverts, or catch woodcock visiting *en route* to their winter home. Aldo Leopold wrote about these special times in his *Sand County Almanac* when he said, "There are two kinds of hunting: ordinary hunting and ruffed grouse hunting," and "There are two times to hunt in Adams County [Wisconsin]: ordinary times and when the tamaracks are smoky gold."

These are days of great anticipation, getting ready to get ready, prepare to prepare, loading and unloading and, finally, you are there, in camp. Up until now, the expected conveniences of modern-day living were readily accessible at home, the restaurant, and the gas station, but now you enter another world, one of a more primitive existence.

But it is in those cabins you find solace and you become closer to the game bird hideouts with your good friends. It is here the dogs can sleep on your bed, on the tired and torn, back-breaking sofa, sit and beg by the table when the food is ready, rush through the barely opened front door and deposit their discomfort anyplace in sight, oftentimes creating a minefield of cautious trespass. It is here that the morning urges turn into fire-hose velocity or tap-water drip from a strategic position on the porch; God help the railing if at a disadvantageous height. But it is No 2, its unforgiving urgency followed by pleasant satisfaction from a regimented visit to the "House Outback" that must preclude any good gunning for the day.

While the colloquially termed outhouse, back-house, privy, or crudely, shit house normally has accessories that are seldom found at Bed Bath & Beyond, they serve the purpose well. Rolled paper is left on end within easy reach, frequently protected inside a coffee can, away from rain and snow. A conventional dispenser is too pricy for this throne room. There's no privacy lock inside, an occupancy notice is verbal and announced definitively inside camp amongst mysterious odors that follow a big breakfast, a good bean supper, or an overdose of canned or bottled alcoholic beverages.

The "house outback" is where one finds welcome relief. It is a significant upgrade from the prickly log of random discovery, where no good library, or paper goods are handy. This respite, often out of level on an uneven rotted foundation is likely to be of elevated single- or two-hole design.

In the corner is a can of lye, a critical ingredient, usually with a small shovel or other like tool to dispense a good measure down the hole, directly on the pyramid to encourage chemical action in the off hours. Sorry, no air freshener here.

Upscale houses sometimes utilize a discarded white toilet seat that was used at home for twenty years but still has some good use left in it, no need for the bolts to fit or hinges to work perfectly. Most of the time, gunners that know of such things are amazed at how accurately sized the hole or holes have been crafted; oblong, rounded edges, and a near perfect fit from front to back allowing the performance of all discharges to be executed with precision, superbly directed, splash guarded exquisitely, and aimed precisely upon a predecessor's tracks.

Unless memory is stirred, maybe it was not part of your keen remembrances of camp life, but given a moment of deep recollection, not for dinner conversation, the time when your urgency bell rang elevated its importance exponentially. Without a thoughtful deposit prior to a great gunning day, you cannot reach the zenith of the sporting experience. Your heart just isn't in it! How many times have you loaded your gun and worked into a great cover, approached a dog on point, or readied for action with wild flushes nearby, when nature takes over and the call of the wild suggests you slip off from the gang, slightly out of eyesight and like a speeding bullet, "drop trou." You should have taken care of business in proper order utilizing the primitive, yet functional conveniences in the "house outback."

Should you tire of that age old, dog-eared library at camp, consider some newcomers that could provide an educational experience for the uninitiated: *How to Shit in the Woods* by Kathleen Meyer and *On Bullshit* by Harry G. Frankfurt or maybe even *Pissing in the Snow and Other Ozark Folktales* by Vance Randolph.

No matter your literary preferences, the unspoken experiences at the end of that little well-worn trail, near that wonderful old cabin, are integral parts of the sporting life. The "house outback" in its many forms and styles is part of camp life. Likely you and I have visited a good many, for official or unofficial business, and we remember them in special private ways, often because of a home-life associated with a hardscrabble youth or just that wonderful old camp experience in our memories. Maybe, just maybe, in the house outback, to quote from Lloyd Alexander's *The Book of Three*, "We learn more by looking for the answer and not finding it than we do from learning the answer itself."

The author's children introduced to the outhouse, often called
"The Throne Room" at Jalbert's Camps, Round Pond, Allagash
River—the same used by Supreme Court Justice O'Douglas,
on his trip with "the old guide" Willard Jalbert in the 1960s

"Sacrete" & Art Wheaton with Parker VHE 20

"Sacrete" in Kennelaire
"Your dog seems a little stiff."

"Sacrete"

Old Pats Society Legendary Rock-solid Pointer

Every bird hunter wants to be proud of his dog. While hunting with friends in the field, you expect the best performance from your trusted companion as it gives credence to good bloodlines, good training, and a great nose. On this occasion, one bird dog distinguished himself from all the rest, with such staunch points, head and tail high, intensity strong, and the classiest of style made famous by his stud book pedigree.

I loaded "Brandy," my English Setter in her "Kennel-Aire" wire dog crate in the back of my red Jeep Cherokee. Most hunters use the fiberglass sky kennel now.

Ken, my long-time friend and hunting partner that day, along with his son, Ken the Third, took what seemed like extra care to assemble an array of stuff: camera, peanut butter crackers, cookies, munch-style snacks, shells, and other miscellaneous gear. We were soon off to meet Mitch in Topsfield, a crossroads oasis comprised of one Irving gas station/convenience store some twenty-five miles away.

Mitch is a local guide, woodsman, and outdoorsman, one of the L. L. Bean or Woolrich green-checked jacket crowd, sometimes claimed as a friend of mine. He was going to take us to some of *his* favorite covers that day. Mitch is infamous for his sense of humor, which includes a repertoire of jokes, pranks, and one-liners typical of a true Mainer. Of course, Mitch was never known to plain lie or fabricate, but he could bend the truth like the flexibility of a 12" elastic rule that could be extended to 14" (the legal length) when a landlocked salmon was netted close to lunch time. His black bears were always bigger than most, his whitetail bucks weighed more and had more points; all this delivered with a straight face, as dry as any "Down-Easter" in the state, and, naturally, dragging the *r*'s.

When we pulled into the gas station, he was waiting in his old, green pick-up truck. Mitch got out and stuck his head in the passenger window next to Ken, twisted his head and peered toward my dog crate in the back.

"Art, your dog seems a little stiff," he said in true Down-Easter style, as he thought my name had six *a*'s and three *r*'s before you got to the *t*. In English class, we might have called it a "long A" like AAAAAArrrt.

"Oh," I replied, "she's not in very good shape, and I probably let her run a little too much yesterday." My dog was a one-week-a-year grouse hunter and not well conditioned for an eight-hour-long day's hunt.

Mitch persisted, with further comment, "Yeaah, but she's not moving around."

"She'll be okay," I said, "as soon as we get into the cover and she gets limbered up." In my mind, I knew "Brandy" could not be pushed hard and she would need a good long noon rest, probably just like me.

This story began one morning in 1995. It is the whole truth and nothing but the truth, I swear! From the best memories of the "Old Pats Society," this is the way it happened.

The day started with a lot of commotion, plenty of scurrying around getting hunting parties organized, like herding chickens: lots of cackling, crowing, and prancing around; going in all directions. Short of using handcuffs and an old-time cattle prod, my attempt to get this crowd moving was modest at best. Coffee cups were refilled, one last donut consumed, just a few more things to load, or you name it. Finally, the threesomes were aligned with "dog power."

Dog expertise was arguable; more a fact of matching a dog, his master, and hunters. Some dogs might even come to the whistle, some responded better from high-volume yelling, or come-a-running after three shots were fired. We did have one dog that recognized the SUV horn as a sign for a dog treat. Oh, I don't mean to say our dogs were unskilled, untrained, or worthless; nah, some really were pretty good bird finders. With some sense of organization, the parties were off.

The three of us met Mitch, who suggested, "Follow me along Route 6, then I'll turn off on a dirt logging road that eventually will split at a spaghetti junction of woods roads, with one terminating on a little birch side hill where there should be some woodcock and grouse." This secret cover took a little finding. If you have never been in the Maine woods after an area had been cut over, you haven't experienced such a chance to lose your way. The maps were not yet updated for these cuttings.

We parked the vehicles in an obvious opening on the edge of the narrow road, slid from the comfort of leather seats, the warm heater, and had one last sip from a stale cup of coffee. I proceeded to the rear of my jeep, grabbed the lift-gate handle, pushed the button, and opened it only to stare eyeball to eyeball with the impassive white-and-black face of a *concrete Dalmatian imposter*, sitting motionless in my crate. He glared at me with unwavering intensity. I stared and he stared back, stoic and proud, not sure what to say. Just a smidge of contempt was evident in the painted eyes, maybe a little resentment from having its head crammed into the cage, pushing the wire mesh roof up about an inch to make room for his height. This dog did not bark, whine, wink, or stir as he stared straight at me. It was obvious there would be no winning the stare down.

"Where the hell is my dog?" I exclaimed, rather indignantly, amidst the roaring laughter and slapping of knees. This planned "sting" was having the desired effect on Mitch, Ken and K-III. It took some time before a calm came over the crowd, all the while the whereabouts of my dog were of no concern to anyone but me. Nobody had a clue where "Brandy" might be, so here we were, ready for a great day in what looked like one of the best covers we might find that week, and no dog except this *spotted cement fire engine mascot*, and he was not moving, had no interest in the alders, and cared less about the levity around him.

Playing along with the joke…what other choice did I have…pictures were taken and we made the best of the morning. We took a turn in this good-looking cover of side-hill birches. It had plenty of soft, dark dirt underneath and was a likely woodcock haven. I vaguely remember a few "air balls" and firing a few shots, but got very little blood in my game bag. Somehow, my heart really wasn't in it with "Brandy" missing. You get used to having your dog out there in front of you, and even though in my youth I had hunted "dogless," once you experience this wonderful sport with a dog at your side, there is no going back. It turned out to be a fine morning, with the sun peeking through those bright birch tops, warming the soil, and taking the crispness out of the air. The day was best memorialized by the photos taken and the joke of all jokes played on me. Not till our lunch rendezvous at Roger's camp did we get Paul Harvey's "The rest of the story…"

The real root of this practical joke apparently began when Chuck Mosher, the "Reverend Leroy," stopped at a local's home on his way from the nearby town of Brookton, twelve miles away, where he proceeded to give a lady four boxes of *my* shotgun shells to "borrow" the Dalmatian lawn ornament for the day. He then arranged to make the switch with "Brandy" that morning, while I was being kept occupied with ineffective prodding of the hunting parties. Little did he know at the time that Darlene, from whom he borrowed the Dalmatian, was in fact the head cook at Wheaton's Lodge, my youngest brother's sporting camp. I was to hear of this practical joke for years thereafter from her as well as from all the Old Pats gang.

It appears the whole scam could not have been carried out without an accomplice, in this case it was William Harnden Foster's grandson, Jon. He acknowledged, "I loaded 'Brandy' in my vehicle, and we were supposed to follow Mitch to that secret cover, holding a good distance back, then to deliver your dog after the joke was over. But the scheme turned sour when we got lost making a series of wrong turns in that maze of woods roads." The lunchtime hilarity gained momentum with each new embellishment, heightened when the cost of this scheme was told: it took four boxes of 8 shot taken from my own private supply, so, in effect, I financed the whole joke. Brookton's finest fire engine guardian, the Dalmatian, was appropriately named "Sacrete" and forever has a spot in the group mug-shot taken at lunch. In the annals of the Old Pats hunts, this practical joke has tickled the uninitiated and seasoned members alike. Just wait, my turn is coming. At the right moment, I plan to strike back and reclaim dignity.

"Sacrete" has returned to duty in his normal spot, rain or shine, winter or summer, guarding that front lawn, having proven his work ethic and outstanding reliability, never to leave his post, remembered forever as a staunch, rock-solid Pointer!

Chuck Mosher, AKA "The Reverend Leroy"; Randy Havel, AKA "The Great Morel"; Tom Larson; and Jerry Havel—"Lunch in the Field," Longville, MN

Tim McKelvey, Ken Waite III, Tim McCormack, Scott Hanes, Raul Benny, Matt Ambrose, and Ken Berger in the Adirondacks, 2016

"Molly" Shane Wheaton's English Pointer

It Don't Get No Better Than This!

My father used what I describe as "country English" to capture a very special moment: "It don't get no better than this!"

In 2011, a hand-framed, 1941 antique calendar of Myron W. Maxim of South Paris, Maine, arrived with the page for April showing the fourth circled in red. On the back, it was inscribed "To Art at Old Pats, Pal, Ken." The Edmund Osthaus image of a Setter with grouse being retrieved says much about wonderful times, but that inscription had deep sentiment. No matter what you choose to call those rare moments, relish and reflect on them as precious gifts that dot the sporting trail of life.

We hunted along the edge of a swale; "Molly," the young Pointer on my left, began making game. Ah, a solid point; the cock lifted and swung out over the back water, colliding with a charge of #8s and dumping right in the water within sight.

"Molly" saw it fall, tested a little of the water half-way to her knees, then with a little encouragement went right up to her stomach to pick up the bird and bring it to hand while my partner, John looked on. *"It don't get no better than this!"*

———

The mule deer were in rut and the nice four-point was hot on a doe. I pulled up to within one hundred yards and watched patiently. "That's your buck," I whispered to my daughter, Heather, who carefully took aim. "Put the cross hairs beneath the chin," I said, then waited, and waited, and waited, an eternity! Finally, the 7mm-08 went off, the buck bolted and collapsed within twenty-five yards; then, the crying began. It was the biggest buck in camp. Her first one ever! *It don't get no better than this!*

———

He waded into the river as I watched from the high bank, casting the fly on a diagonal, gently edging further into the river so the fly would sweep across the current just below the submerged rock. That obstacle caused the rushing water to part, making for an Atlantic salmon lie along the current line. My son took a quick suggestion to move a bit further out, lengthen the cast so as to reach just the right spot. From the dark water, the salmon struck, leaped and ran off fifty yards of line, the swift water its helper. A couple more jumps, some hair-raising runs and thirty minutes later the fish idled to the little eddy while Dad and pride witnessed landing his very first Atlantic. "*It don't get no better than this!*"

———

We all sat around the table, old friends and Old Pats Society pals for thirty years or more. Next to it, the old woodstove was freshly stoked with dry rock maple, the chill now gone from our rainy day in the covers. No birds and everybody got soaked. Now our glasses were being tipped, sipping celebratory libation in the form of a little warm brandy, some smooth Tennessee whisky, or fine single malted barley, all of which sharpen the brain cells of perfect recall. Our exploits together: the scams, the many tricks, the good food, the good guns, the dogs, and above it all the underlying fabric of long-lasting friendship. As time slips away and the shadows grow longer for us, we step back in our minds, then and now, thankful of our good fortunes, because "*It don't get no better than this!*"

―――――

One late October morning found my son and I in an alder and apple tree cover, the dog casting off to the left while a nice grouse was running ahead on the ground, suggesting that a move wide to the right might encourage her to move left and ultimately flush in front of my son. He was carrying my old Parker VHE 20 that I recently had given him. The cover ended at the field edge just ahead so that bird had no place to go. Then, like a grand plan, the bird sensed it was trapped and took to the air to collide sharply with a cloud of 8s, becoming the very first bird my son would take with that favorite old gun. "*It don't get no better than this!*"

―――――

In the early evening in the lobby of the Mahaffey Theatre in St. Petersburg, Florida, my father said to his friend, "We'll go up in the balcony." He slid in beside Bud Brooks, in the front row seats looking down when the "Tennessee ploughboy" took his stool at center stage. The lights had dimmed and the spots focused on the famous crooner, Eddie Arnold, as he sang a couple of familiar tunes, then launched into the old favorite…" Anytime you're feeling lonely, anytime you're feeling blue." My father had settled in comfortably; then leaned over, nudged his old friend with his left elbow and whispered softly, *'It don't get no better than this!"*

―――――

Now in the twilight of an upland shooting life, like an old dog who lies around, sleeps a lot, and remembers his staunch points, I like to think about those special moments and especially Dad at the Mahaffey…"*It don't get no better than this!*"

Art Wheaton, Randy Havel, and Chuck Mosher on a great morning with Parker 28 gauges

The Times

With more age around the eyes, more silver in the hair, and the hills steeper, comes wisdom...

It's not all about the birds, It's about the TIMES!

I t was not always that way. When the fever of youth ran high—boundless energy forever in the tank and limits on our mind—the thickets, tangles, and terrain were a mere inconvenience. We took to the covers before the sun warmed the slopes and closed the day when the last bird lifted, fleeting against a twilight sky. No time to waste at a diner, our lunch consisted of a sandwich, cookie or candy bar, and an apple in our game pocket. Oh, what grand days they were.

Gene Hill wisely told us, "Our greatest trophies are not things, but *times*." For it is those *times* we will remember forever, savoring the special moments, telling the old stories over again, reliving those yesterdays as, like a good stew, the taste gets better after a few days.

Budget-minded trophies decorated our dens. A simple gray or brown fan pinned on cardboard, salted with a dash of borax to dry the flesh-tipped feathers was bona fide evidence of shooting prowess. Great shots were vividly remembered, missed shots too, often excused while we debated the virtues of Express 7½s vs. 8s, pigeon loads, nickel shot, copper coated shot, spreader loads, and high or low brass. Like a stringer of fish, the epitome of success was to "limit out."

High flush counts are important, great for the diary, but "shootable birds" were never defined from out-of-sight wingbeats. Bragging rights gleaned from photo-ops were of great importance. Pictures were taken of birds on trunks, on vests, logs, back-dropped against productive covers. Those pictures captured our dogs and guns and vehicles and Scottish hats, baseball caps and Old Pats inscribed blaze orange hats…all part of the fading treasure trove of the past.

And then, as if by magic, a gray-haired graduation occurred as we had forgotten a good bit about all those birds, who shot what, and who limited out. Details, many fleeting, remembered with often fuzzy detail were stirred from amongst a shoebox of photos, making those seemingly less important things more important now. Great days of the past were better remembered and illuminated from the memories of those kindred spirits pictured.

The shadows today grow longer, in the twilight of a wonderful sporting life, when, as we gather next to a crackling fire, fingers grip gently around a partially filled, etched-glass tumbler, while someone lights a cigar. The conversation warms to, "Remember when…" and invariably, the stories told reveal more about old and precious *times* than birds.

There were good *times* with gun dogs, the part they played to etch their names into our memories. They are with us but a short while, having painted pictures in our minds of special moments, some great, some sad, some good, some bad. Without such accompaniment the band could not have played those sweet songs of yesterday. Bill Tarrant in *Field & Stream* (1983) said it quite well:

Old gun dogs have stood the test of time and event and circumstance. They come now, slowly, and lay at foot or close to side, jowls flat, eyes faded with the fog of cataract, their muzzles and paws white or speckled salt and pepper. But they come. They want to be close. They are great treasures, these old dogs. For they are more than themselves lying there. They are us.

There were good times using, admiring, and talking about our chosen tools of the trade. It began with 12-gauge "brush busters," Model 32s, Parker 12s, and then almost daringly the 20-gauge 1100 autoloader and 870 pump sneaked into our repertoire; quietly, gently, occasionally, thinking all the time, "We *really* did not want to miss." The 20s, lighter and a little quicker, gradually became the preferred, as now with little concern for bag limits but more on quality of experience, a seemingly fairer chase, we revel in traditions gleaned from Spiller, Foster, Sheldon, and Ford, who told us about apple orchards, birch knolls, alder runs, and creeks meandering through farm pastures. They taught us to play the game. Nowadays, as we begin the "back nine," some still prefer light 20s, but it is the 28 that has become a favorite.

Choice guns were selected for their American soul, for America's greatest gamebirds…Parkers, L. C. Smith, Ithaca, Lefever and Fox, Browning or Remington, Stevens or Ithaca, or some other favorite. More than ever we cherish those choices. To shoulder, point, clean, wipe, oil, grease, and admire, our guns provide an indescribable comfort, a special pleasure and connection to this world. These priceless things, not to be sold or traded, live with us until the end, then, and only then, go on to a worthy proud steward. We are blessed with having had such chances, thinking and hoping that we can still do it again, all the time wondering how it got so late, and so soon?

There were good times laced with humor, like the emergency when the truck came to a screeching halt. I bolted from the cab, leaving the engine running, while you watched me with elbows slashing, vanishing, as I slipped just out of sight into the woods, to return, absent my shorts, personal comfort restored. Then who could forget about "Sacrete" the rock-solid Pointer/Dalmatian that replaced "Brandy" in my crate.

There were special times like that late afternoon cover in Minnesota, you wing tipped a grouse, a left-to-right crosser, that broke through a window of opportunity. The dog found him, and then you stoned a riser on the way out of the cover with your Parker DHE 28, claiming you just really wanted to "fringe" the first one…albeit good shots and a special time.

Then do you recall the time you tripped and fell against a rock, gouging the wood on your fine Parker 28 gauge and when you shipped your Parker to Maine in advance, and we carefully unwrapped it, substituting a single barrel beater, then watched your color turn white, an expression of great concern, never connecting pranksters to the crime. Long ago we made the great trade of my father's old Oneida Community #4 Bear Trap that was hanging in our big pine tree for a 1911 Bristol steel fishing rod poster titled "A Tragedy" by Oliver Kemp…I still have that poster. And what about those great "in the field" lunches we had, when you brought that wooden table and folding chairs, the smoked canned oysters, sardines, and crackers, and we told stories. And that late cool fall when I pulled my Parker 20 Trojan from its case in the back of the station wagon to learn the stock was split at the wrist and when your Setter swam the creek to get that downed grouse on the other side. Then there was the time you arranged for George Flaim to mount those two great mature grouse, one gray and one brown, heads cocked, fanned ruffs and tails in a full strut; both shot in midwinter, each one had broken my way as we tramped through the heavy snow. Little did we know that years would slip away quietly, like a fall breeze, and that we would really become *Old* Pats.

Do you remember the woodcock that bounced off my gun barrel, grabbing for air, in his haste to leave the scene of surprise, or those great walleye dinners we had at Patrick's in Longville, and the mixed double you shot in Maine? Remember when it snowed in late October and we had to use the chainsaw on that tree that fell across the road leaving camp, then tramped in the wet, snow-covered evergreens most of the morning, getting soaked to the skin.

What was most often full was not our game bags, but our memories that now runneth over. We reflect and know the birds just provided the frosting, while the cake was composed of old friends, trips and times together.

When you come to the end of the long, long trail,

And your hunting and trapping days are gone,

When your step grows weak and your sinews fail,

And it's time to answer the great last call;

It isn't the size of the cabin you've built,

Nor what you have won in pelts or fame,

The thing that counts is the right to say

"I have kept the faith—I have played the game."

Albert M. Ahearn, 1922

Now, another October is here, "the creeks did not rise and the lord was willing." Now we have that chance to do it all again, to glimpse a woodcock settle in a patch of alders, watch a grouse flush from under an old apple tree, but especially, it will be a reunion, to have new *times*, have laughter, bask in the camaraderie, have gun talk, dog talk, and share fond moments again, with and about friends, some departed. We will craft new lyrics, polish the pitch, rhythm, and harmony to make a sweet melody out of these *times*. For I know, in the end, it will always be about you and me and when we will be together again, because you just can't make old *friends* and you just can't make old *times*.

Bill Hamilton's "Woodrow", the wonder dog

The Reverend Leroy bakes rolls, 1997

OVER "JUST COFFEE AND A PIECE OF PIE"...
We Were Young, Once Again

The Suburban came to a stop about 10:30 that morning and we entered "The Mill-yard," a local convenience store, logging-truck gas stop, and restaurant, walked past the pastry rack and counter stools, and squeezed into an end booth. The waitress came over, took one look and commented, "You might be more comfortable at the table in the other room." She wisely sensed our bulk needed space and redirected us through the double doors to the empty room and a long table just inside, Dr. Waite settling into the end seat.

"What can I get for you," she said.

"Oh, did I see pie?" Tim replied.

"Yes, our pies are homemade," she answered.

"I'll have *just coffee and a piece of pie*," said Tim.

"Me, too," piped in Randy, and Ken chimed in with the same.

It seemed too early for lunch, too late for breakfast, but we had chosen not to hunt that morning, just visit together, talk and reminisce over the old days, enjoying long-lasting friendships.

While our coffee cups were kept full, we stepped back across the threshold of time to become *young once again*. Once faded memories were sharpened when collaborative recollections illuminated the details of real-life stories, for it is those stories that live on.

———

"There's an awful lot of smoke for God's sake," someone said.

Then Scott Hanes chimed in, "There's a fire in the oven," as a layer of black smoke enveloped the whole cabin. The Reverend Leroy had decided to make rolls but got distracted in lively conversation, a single malt Scotch, and feeding his dog, "Amos." He used the special recipe for the store-bought rolls Ken had bought—just unwrap, heat, and serve. We gasped for air when the oven was opened, to learn that the finish on Gram's (belonging to my eighty-nine-year-old mom) fine serving tray that had been used to heat up his rolls now had fire lapping along its sides and was being burned to a crisp. The Reverend said, "It was all Lance's fault for leaving the tray out." Mom's fancy painted tray was completely ruined, our rolls had been permeated with paint, a kerosene-like smell, and smoke, left unfit for consumption. Chuck said, "I never ate rolls again." The tray, like a burned-out car, remains a wall ornament with a picture of Chuck and "Amos" glued to the middle, permanently hung in the Old Pats clubhouse.

Randy said, "Remember when we were staying at Bowen Lodge on Big Winne, Lake Winnebegosh in Minnesota? There Ken would say as we entered a local pie and coffee shop, 'You won't see that "Welcome Hunters" sign around Connecticut.'" That's the trip where Chuck, Ken, Randy, Tim, Tom Larson, and I hunted some fire lanes, strips of land that had been cut and were one hundred yards long of five-to-seven-year-old aspen. A woodcock broke, Tim pulled up, missed, but on a re-flush connected. He was the only one to shoot and the bird fell, stone dead, directly under the front bumper of our station wagon. Tim quipped, "I was careful to calculate my shot path before pulling the trigger so that it would just clear the front windshield."

———

Chuck reminded us of "Woodrow," fondly called the Wonder Dog, a fantastic English Setter owned by Honorable Old Pats member, Bill Hamilton.

He said, "I never saw that dog run. I followed him once on a running grouse for at least twenty minutes before that bird finally made the mistake of trying to hide in a brush pile. He never pushed them hard and never lost his focus. When you walked behind him you KNEW who was in charge of that hunt. In a breed prized for dignity and calm composure, he was the James Earl Jones of Setters."

"Hey," Tim said, "What about the year we had the country music band and they could not get enough of your free whisky all evening? So, when they left, one fella told us, 'Think I will have a roady' and proceeded to fill his giant 7-11 marked cup to the brim with Crown Royal. You would have been better to fill the gallon of Crown with Four Roses."

Randy followed again with his recollections of when we hunted "the Cemetery Cover" in Minnesota, where only old growth and distant memories now survive.

———

It was a place where no one ever bothered to traipse the fifty yards along the fence line border of that little stone village to get to the best part. Those long-deceased residents watched from their place markers: Carlson, Thompson, Knutson, Erickson, or Swenson. It could have been difficult to find that cover again, but Randy had driven me right to it one day a year earlier. The best part began just out of sight of the road, behind the village, and was bordered by a field on the left, then a creek bed with a dike bulldozed for flood control and about a mile back an old road became the cover terminus. Randy reminded me, "My old 'Lucy' the black lab flushed a grouse out of a dead fall, the bird quartered left as I fired across about four inches of snow topping that open field, with the bird headed for some oaks on the other side. At the shot, with wings locked, it scaled for sixty yards seeming to light in the refuge of an oak savannah. Art, you remember, after considerable debate as to whether it was hit, we walked over and found the bird stone dead, splayed, with wings spread out in the snow." Now we always follow up on a shot.

Randy reminded us again, "Do you remember in Floodwood, Minnesota, when Ron Sanders, a fine bird hunter who has now crossed that great divide, took us to his very own secret cover? We trudged a mile and half hike down a two-track dike. A big dead hickory tree was on our left and a grouse went up. Dr. Waite killed it instantly; then another jumped, someone else killed it and then another, then another. Now with four in the bag, the last trailing bird narrowly escaped amongst a fusillade of fine shot, when Ronnie said, 'And we haven't even reached my honey hole!"

Ken added, "How about our trip to Palmquest's farm in Wisconsin? We laughed into the night in the log cabin, enjoyed family style dining, and listened to 'Rip-Roaring Ryan'—'the judge'—who bragged to us about his newly acquired and well-trained Setters. The next day as he took his whistle, the dogs were armored up with the latest in beepers and shock collars, then turned loose in a likely cover." Again Ken reminded us, "Soon the beeping faded, the 'come heres' became elevated to the highest pitch of an opera soprano, while the intensity of the shocking collar increased supposedly commensurate with the applied thumb pressure. The pair disappeared and were not to be seen again for the rest of the morning."

Now, with the gray in our thinning hair and the light dimming in once keen eyes, time has slipped away, albeit softly, like an unintelligible whisper, making those now overgrown, barely discernable, distant old roads of no return more precious than ever. It may be time for us to take Will Roger's sage advice, "We can really slow the aging process down by running it through Congress."

We remain grateful for our generous book of stories that are the fabric that indelibly links us forever. It is that glue of friendship that has allowed us to make such memories, now it is the telling of those stories, over and over again, like the warp and weft of a loom, woven into our sporting life. That trail of stories lives in our hearts and minds; those moments too precious to forget, because each sporting experience of our lives is made legitimate by the story that grows from it, and without that special story, the experience is meaningless or long forgotten.

That morning, over *just coffee and a piece of pie*, we looked back for a fleeting moment, with the comfort, caring, and the excitement of those precious old times, when we were young once again.

Ken Berger & Fox A-grade 16 gauge

Fox in the Henhouse

Roger worked the crowd for a sense of what his little side-by-side 16-gauge Fox shotgun might bring—he must have been a little short this month. *Who* among his friends would provide the best estimate of value, or even suggest what he could sell it for?

From the *Gun Traders Guide* to the *Blue Book of Gun Values* to our most experienced Old Pats gun show traders, the estimates of value ranged from $600 to $1,500. But there were no takers. Roger said he would like to sell; understood was the unspoken word that he would also like to get top dollar. But he was in the company of some pretty shrewd gun folks. The inevitable discussion of pricing went on, obviously tilted toward whether you were buying or selling. The talk was fun and the banter lively. Roger knew he would have difficulty finding a qualified buyer once he got back home.

Then, in the waning hours, before our annual Old Pats Society hunt ended, Ken Berger, our chef, offered up $1,500, cash money.

He told Roger that the gun required a new stock made to modern dimensions, which would turn it into a good shooting grouse gun. "And not just any restocking would do," he said. "No, sir, a good restocking job would duplicate the original checkering style and pattern, with a finish to look like the original, and be a perfect fit to the frame." It was a job for an expert craftsman. That could cost thousands.

Not long after Ken returned to his home in Ohio, the phone rang and he picked up. It was Roger: "Would you give me $1,800 for the gun, Ken?"

"I can't do that, Roger," he said. "You know what needs to be done to that gun. Once I have is restocked I'll have more invested in it than it's worth."

A week later Roger called again. He announced that he had decided to reduce his price to $1,700. He was privately sure that Ken really wanted the gun and would be willing to up his offer. Ken held his ground. About ten days later another telephone call from Roger resulted in a small further reduction in price.

"Let's stop beating around the bush," Ken said. "As I offered once before, I'll send you a check tomorrow for $1,500."

Roger paused. "Okay, you have a deal, but I still think the price is too low."

The acquisition of a fine side-by-side shotgun is always fodder for members of the Old Pats Society to gather around, expressing collective *ooohs* and *aaahs* over the finer points of such a find. Some mighty fine Parker, L. C. Smith, Baker, or Fox shotguns have found their way into another already bulging gun safe this way. *Want* generally surpasses *need* on a gun deal.

This story really began when our favorite Mainer, "Roger-the-Dodger," discovered this nice little Fox 16 gauge. It was a lightweight A-grade, had a small 20-gauge frame and, by any measure, felt and handled more like a 20 than a 16. The splinter forend, 26-inch barrels, slim stock and frame all screamed quick handling, easy and light to carry: an ideal bird gun. But— usually there's a but in gun trading—the small, delicate stock had horrible shooting dimensions by today's standards. It had a three-inch drop at the heel, one and three-quarter at the comb, and had been shortened to 13 inches' length of pull. The case color of the frame, barrel bluing, and wood finish were in the 80 percent range, making it a very attractive gun, but… One must remember this gun probably was built in the early 1900s yet did not show the wear usually associated with guns of that age. It may have been purchased particularly for a lady, youngster, or someone slight of build. We will never know. Speculation always abounds as to whether a gun was built initially that way or if it was later altered to suit someone else, begging the question, is it original or not?

It seems Roger purchased this gun from a "lead" given him by a business colleague. Digging deep into a hidden can, buried somewhere in his yard most likely, he extracted a secret stash of $200 and hesitantly coughed it up to buy the little Fox. Now, Roger was never known to spend many hard Yankee dollars for a shotgun. He must have been given encouragement from "on high" to complete that transaction. It sat squirreled away in his closet until that October and then was brought out at the Old Pats traditional lobster dinner and gun show.

For the unknowing non-members, our "gun show" is highly informal. It's a forum for returning members to display their wares, some of which were acquired over the past year and some that had never been displayed at the show. It simply is the adult version of show and tell. Gun folks love to talk about their stuff, relish in the find, and brag a little. You know the drill: about the little old lady who drove her prized possession only on sunny days; further touting the game of, "I have it and you can't buy it." Our version is more like: "Take a look at this nice piece I just found. Look at the condition. Heft it, point it, but don't ding it—it ain't for sale, maybe."

Ken's check for $1,500 was in the mail but the cat-and-mouse game continued. It seems Roger's house number had changed and Ken had sent his check to an obsolete address. Waiting and waiting for the promised check made Roger only more anxious. Had Ken changed his mind? Roger called Ken. Yes, of course, he still wanted the gun and would immediately send a duplicate check.

The gun finally arrived at its new home. Ken then proceeded to engage a highly competent gunsmith, with instructions to duplicate the stock as original as possible in fit and finish, but with dimensions taken from his old Parker 16-gauge grouse and woodcock "rain" gun. He had utmost confidence with that old gun, had dispatched many a bird in years past with it, and he knew he would have a grouse-killing machine once the work on the Fox was completed.

Fast forward to that next Old Pats hunt the following year. The members, as you can imagine, had all heard chapter and verse of Roger's big gun sale. Under the word "tight" in the dictionary, Roger is pictured. Having grown up as a frugal Yankee, he is most careful of his expenses, measuring money carefully, like a spoonful of sugar. It has always been a stretch for him to spend a couple of hundred dollars for a gun purchase. We all knew this. You see, Roger put his two kids though fine New England schools at the University of Maine and Middlebury College. It is in his DNA knowing how hard money is to get. Once obtained it is not easy for him to part with it.

The curtain came up on the next year's Old Pats gun show night. This was a time of high spirits and anticipation, always filled with excitement for a peek at new temptations. What will show up, what will come sliding out of those canvas gun slips, those leg-o-mutton leather cases, trunk cases, or plain old cheap cloth gun covers? As we have all seen, a gun's case may or may not be a clue to the find of the century—but it sure whets the appetite when an old leather-strapped Abercrombie & Fitch trunk with brass hardware, leather corners, terribly worn at the strap creases, leather cracked and faded, is paraded into the room.

The story of Roger's A-grade Fox had spread far and wide, even to four directors of the Parker Gun Collectors Association. These invited guests were basking in the levity and camaraderie of the evening, eager to see what would be unveiled for the eye to behold, maybe even what might be for sale. It was Roger's first introduction to these gun-trading aficionados. Wisps of blue cigar smoke hovered over the crowd. Half-filled glasses of amber enlightenment were held by every hand.

As prized Parkers were pulled from their cases—or a Fox, L. C. Smith, or some intriguing specimen with which we were unfamiliar, was brought to the party—the critiques ranged from serious to humorous. Remember, one can't brag up a gun too much if you have interest; the price might inflate beyond reach.

Finally, it was Ken's turn for show and tell. Out came the lovely little Fox, all dressed in her new stock. The gun was quickly passed around for admiration and a hoist to the shoulder with all keen eyes on the finished stock work. Then it was Charlie Herzog's turn to look her over.

"Nice gun," Charlie said. "I have always liked these little 16-gauge Fox guns."

"Handles real nice," Ken piped in. "Now it fits me like my old Parker. Should be real sweet coming up in thick cover."

"Is it for sale?" Charlie asked. "I always wanted one for my son."

"Naw," Ken replied. "I just got it fixed up! Haven't even hunted with her yet."

"Come on," Charlie said. "Everything is for sale. What would it really take to buy this gun, Ken? Name your price."

"Charlie, I don't have any intention of selling it," Ken responded flatly.

"Ken," Charlie said, "I'll offer you $6,000 for this gun right now. I'll write you a check on the spot. It is just the gun my son wants and it will fit him just great," he added, reaching for his back pocket.

Ken thought a few minutes.

"Charlie," he finally said, "I don't want to sell this gun. But in reality, I don't really need it. I have a couple of Parkers and two or three other doubles to shoot."

All the while, Roger was sitting in the corner relishing a fine cigar and listening to the exchange. When the offer of $6,000 surfaced, he stood up to get a better look at his old gun and be closer to the action, taking another puff from one of those special Top Stone cigars brought from Connecticut by Jim Ryan. Roger had found the box and was working through his fair share of the "community" property.

The seriousness of the negotiation heated up. Charlie commenced to embellish his "need" by suggesting this would be wonderful for his son who had a bit of a handicap. Now he voiced what appeared on the surface to be a heightened plea. The negotiation turned into action. The play was now in its third act. Charlie reached for his checkbook as the audience observed Ken's attachment for the gun weakening. Roger tightened his teeth on his cigar.

"Hell," Ken announced, "if you really want it that bad, you can have it."

"Thanks a lot, Ken, I appreciate it" said Charlie. He pulled his checkbook from his back pocket and laid it down on the table. "Anyone have a pen?"

Roger coughed. I thought I saw some of the blood drain from his face as he slipped out the door to inhale some cool air. He had just watched his $200 bargain Fox A-grade on which he made a tidy sum of $1,300 profit resold for $6,000. Ken, of course, had invested another grand or so in stock work but would line his pocket with a cool $3,700. Roger had naturally done the simple math in his head while the transaction took place. It was too much for him to stand and he slipped outside.

It was all the rest of us could do to hold back the laughter. Jim Baker came in from outside and reported that Roger looked like someone sizing his mouth for a 9 mm.

We invited Roger back in to an eruption of laughter.

Of course, the scam had been carefully set in place before the gun show. Getting Charlie on board as a "surprise buyer" and guest of the Old Pats Society made it all the more believable. Reluctantly he had agreed to go along with the plan only after our assurances that he wouldn't really end up shelling out the $6,000 for a new gun.

The finely refurbished Fox A-grade now rests in Ken's gun vault while Roger remains highly suspicious of this gun-trading crowd. The scam will always be remembered as "the Fox in the Henhouse."

"The corduroy road cover"—Minnesota
(Rear left to right) The Admiral, Tom Larson, Ken Waite Jr.,
Vic Romano Jr., (front) Pete Jackson, "Scotch," "Lucy," Art Wheaton

A great day in Minnesota with the retrieving
by Pete Jackson's labrador

Captain Jim Ryan, Parker DHE 20

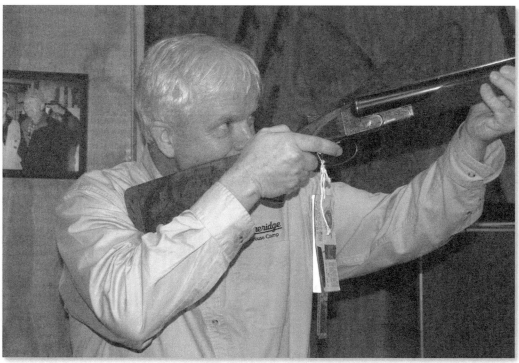
Fred Stump, Ithaca 10 gauge

Taking Stock

When the long winter months are upon us and there're no open seasons now to burn some powder, it is a good time to take out that favorite gun and do a little homework. A satisfying cure for the infection of cabin fever.

"Operator error" is the familiar catch-all phrase for a damn, plain-old miss. I've done it many times and will do it some more before the dirt nap. But, did we learn anything, or just go on our merry way chalking it up to some convenient excuse?

I make no pretense of knowing all the answers to always connecting on flushed birds, but a lot of expended shotgun shells have helped me better understand some things. Gunners come in a variety of sizes: short, tall, long arms, long necks, short necks, and on and on. Also, there are many different styles of shooting. A few observations about gun fit might be helpful in dispatching "ol' ruff" the next time he makes his getaway.

Conventional wisdom says do a little homework to determine your gun stock dimensions. There are some great tools these days to check the LOP (length of pull), DAC (drop at comb), and DAH (drop at heel), but you can do a fair job with a good long straight yardstick or a straight edge and fine ruler. If you want to go to the expense of ordering some good measuring tools, try the Robert Louis Company (1-800-979-9156) or Galazan (1-860-225-6561). A simple way is for one to lay the gun on its rib, upside down on a flat table (you may want to use the edge of a table and alongside the bead sights, not on them) to take the drop measurements. Just measure from table to top of comb and heel.

Short of being professionally measured, find the gun you shoot the best and do some rudimentary measuring, then, write it all down. In fact, do it for all your shotguns to compare the findings from the best shooter to others in the cabinet. It's not such a mystery to find out what is most comfortable to you, but remember to put on the clothes you normally wear in the fall. Throw the gun up at that imaginary bird on the wall. Do it few times with eyes closed; then open them once you have the gun in place. Don't keep messing around and adjusting that gun to your shoulder once it's mounted. You are not going to do that on a fast-moving target next fall. You will want to have the gun come to the shoulder easily (again, with the proper clothes on), so you don't push it away when a stock is too long or pull it in with your thumb against your nose when it's too short.

I have listened to all the pundits and watched them run off a negative barrage when a fine gun shows up with a 13½" to near 14" LOP. It would suit me fine, as I know with my long underwear top, chamois shirt, maybe a light wool vest or an orange shooting vest on, it works for me. Of course, my 32–33" sleeve and 5' 8" height is part of the equation. But you've got to find out what works for you by bringing that gun to your face without a shoulder adjustment. You have to be looking right down the barrel or barrels so the only movement left is to point the gun correctly at or pass through the moving target. The eyes must not see too much rib, indicating the shot will be high, or look at the back of the receiver for the opposite result.

Sure, some folks learn to shoot a particular gun well and that's fine, but others are looking for the best dimensions for them. The opportunity to dispatch some woodcock and grouse this fall may depend on learning a little more of what works best for you.

I have shot at many clay targets and learned a great deal on the trapline. When a few more pounds fatten the cheek, when you mount and shoot the gun 100 or 200 times, you pay attention to sight picture, because that's a game of miss and out. But remember, that's from a mounted gun position. You must have the same sight picture every time you place the stock to your face. Note I said bring the gun to your face and shoulder, not forcing the face down to touch the wood of an improperly mounted gun. The gun should fit nicely in the pocket of your shoulder created by lifting your elbow to a horizontal position. Try it! You will quickly see the difference compared to a gun on the shoulder with no real pocket formed as a gun rest with the elbow at your side.

Once you have your favorite gun in hand, the one you have confidence in, take it to the skeet field or sporting clays range and approximate actual hunting clothing when you shoot. Now most folks shoot round after round of 25, continually having trouble with a particular target. Do something different this time out. Go when you are not pressured to move to the next station. Take a few boxes of shells and stay on that particularly troublesome station. Have someone pull targets for you, maybe get a little help but learn to break that target so it becomes a fixture in your mind. Shoot a case of shells if that's what it takes, but get it right. Going round and round the semi-circle or to the end of the course, breaking all those familiar ones over and over doesn't help to overcome a problematical target. You must take a moment to think carefully why you miss one in particular. Getting the right gun mount, sight picture, and lead will help your odds next fall.

My key field learning came from an old Parker VHE ²⁰⁄₂₆. I bought it from a guy at a trap shoot—silver receiver, banged up stock, and double triggers. No collector gun for sure, but I had it restocked with a plain old straight-grain piece of walnut. The dimensions made for me at 13½" LOP, 1⅝" DAC, 2⅜" DAH, and when done it looked just like an original stock. Then one day, the late Howard Miller put in his famous Miller single trigger. The chokes are near cylinder at .005 right bbl and .006 in left. I wouldn't trade it or sell it for anything, as it was a grouse getter for me. Continued success spells confidence, confidence, and more confidence!

Then what did I do? Found a Parker VHE 28-gauge skeet gun that proved to have dimensions of 13 ⅞" LOP, 1 ⁹⁄₁₆" DAC, and 2 ⁷⁄₁₆" DAH. It also works being pretty darn well, but it was hard to give up the old 20 as the "go to" gun.

This new gun is a hair longer and a little straighter, with a ¹⁄₁₆ less drop at the comb and ¹⁄₁₆ more drop at the heel. Having shot a lot of trap, I like a fairly straight gun. With no intention of altering an original Parker stock, I found the difference to be very insignificant. Slight variations to DOC/DOH may not impact your shooting like LOP, quite important where a 14–15" stock may be the answer for a tall, long-armed gunner.

On another outing, I found myself with another Parker DHE 20 with a 14¼" stock. It was a chore pushing the gun out and away from my shoulder and, even with some success, I missed a number of birds when the gun wasn't mounted properly. Forcing the gun to my shoulder, catching on my clothes during gun mount was unsatisfactory. It was a matter of forcing a sight picture rather than doing it automatically.

Your particular style of shooting is certainly a factor for you. Do you cheek the gun tightly, just touch it to your cheek, or look over the barrels like the old timers who held their heads up straight and liked a lot of drop? As opposed to my trapshooting days when the gun was mounted before calling for a target, I am likely to snap shoot at birds in heavy cover. There's no time to adjust and the gun better come up right, so that it points where you are looking.

Magic answers for a miss are like the magic bullet…there ain't any! But a gun that is a natural extension of you can make considerable difference. When you find the right combination, stick with it.

Many things will cause folks to miss, but the rudimentary basics of good gun pointing are more important than you think. We used to use the old cliché, "wood to wood," meaning the cheek must be on the stock when you pull the trigger. New stock dimension will not solve fundamental errors in gun mount, BUT it will surely help if you give careful study to it and spend some time testing.

Here's another revelation! Highly figured wood doesn't make it point any better. Great in the gun cabinet—I might add, great to show to friends and what a selling point at a gun show—but it doesn't really help in gun pointing.

Ken Waite Jr. & Ken Waite III

Ken Waite Jr. & Chuck Mosher

The Good Doctor

A Tribute to Kenneth N. Waite Jr.

*Most of us just pass through this life with only a few making
notable marks of accomplishment or distinction, leaving
behind a few memorable lasting impressions amongst
a related or social circle, soon to be lost in succeeding
generations. The precious, intimate stories we treasure
are never left as an epitaph in that stone village.*

Once upon a time, the everyman's gunner's bible, the *Shotgun News*, was the monthly newspaper for bargains of rare and hard-to-find guns. *Outdoor Life* and *Field & Stream* whetted one's appetite with stories of faraway places like adventures in Alaska, the Rockies, those fish-and-game-rich destinations of Maine, and a wish list of other wonderful places. Our heroes—Warren Page, Elmer Keith, Jack O'Conner, and others—planted the seeds for a great Sporting Life. It was with those glorious pages open that we met at Ft. Dix, New Jersey, one Saturday morning, talking about dreamed adventures.

He loved guns, worked summer jobs at America's Oldest Gunmaker, an easy commute from his Monroe, Connecticut, home, in an old 1964 Ford Galaxy kept in working repair by his brother, Jim, with weekend plans often disrupted by younger sister, Wendy. He trained his first English Pointer, "Ox," found enough ammunition to ravage the crows in the Monroe, Trumbull, and Easton dumps, chased grouse nearby off Lebanon Road, the Naugatuck State Forest, and the grounds of Fairfield County Fish & Game Club. That was the same place he shot his first-owned, 16-gauge Ranger Shotgun, scoring 17 or 18. As he was walking off, Earl Larson asked, "Ever shoot a Model 32?"

"Nope," he replied.

"Here try mine," offered the man.

"But I don't have any shells," he answered, the one box of 16s being all he could afford each week.

"I have a box for you," the gentleman chimed in.

He then ran his first 25 straight. Those were the days when it was popular to shoot skeet Tuesday and Thursday evenings in Shelton with weekends at the Remington Gun Club in Lordship, Stratford, Connecticut, off Long Island Sound.

A consummate trader, accumulator, and collector, the beginning tutorial was when he sold a set of Sharpe's gauges, found in a pile of sawdust by his father (a carpenter by trade), for a goodly sum. Most of us would have thrown them away. His quest for collectables, sporting art, decoys, shotguns, and arms and ammunition memorabilia found him at gun shows far and wide—the Maryland Arms Show, Brimfield, and Springfield—developing a network of likeminded folks. Over the years, he amassed an outstanding collection of Stratford school decoys and New England shorebirds, as well as rare and impossible-to-find original, early pre-1940 *Arms and Ammunition* posters and calendars. He was a literal walking encyclopedia of their history, value, and rarity, never withholding with such sage advice as, "Quality maintains itself," and, if in doubt, "Your eye will tell you if it's good."

With the patience of Job, he lived large, the perfect gentleman at all times, full of generosity. A promise you could always take to the bank became his value system through a long forty-year Remington career—rising to a Northeast Regional Manager, then partnering with Tom Larson in their own rep business, Stonewood, LLC. He kept trading/

buying collectables into retirement, ever honing his innate skills, "the art of the deal." It was he who usually laughed last when he purchased an item believed to be overpriced. He was a regular at the Grand American Trapshooting Tournament, the S.H.O.T. Show, tried driven birds in Scotland, was an accomplished fly fisherman, made a number or trips to Quebec for Atlantic salmon, and loved bugging for bass.

As a founding member of The Old Pats Society, he hunted the flatlands of Minnesota and Wisconsin in the late 1970s and early 1980s, but ultimately Maine became the regular Old Pats destination, generating a long and treasured list of rich stories, scams, gun trades, and hunting exploits. Many tales featuring the Good Doctor appeared in *Ruffed Grouse Society Magazine*, like "The Sliver Setter," "Do you Remember….Old Pal," "Sacrete: the Rock-solid Pointer," "Lucille" and "Over, 'Just Coffee and a Piece of Pie': We Were Young Once Again." Others appeared in the *Double Gun Journal* ("The President's Parker," "Working Guns Along the Tidewater") or in *Parker Pages* ("A Sportsman's Trademark"). While not the talent of Ben Ames Williams, writing about his favorite subject—Chet MCausland of Fraternity Village—I found the Good Doctor provided endless fodder for fact-based storytelling.

Somebody called him one day and said, "Are you really a doctor?"

"Naw," he said, "he just writes it that way." A licensed practitioner of healing literally, probably not, but one who could always add something for a desired effect, one who was always there as a sounding board, a confidant, so be it "The Good Doctor."

As a double gun aficionado his first Parker was a 12-gauge No 2 frame VH gun with a Beavertail forend that was revitalized from the $200 rack (which, by the way, is all that could be afforded at the time.) He later often used his 12-gauge Fox HE with XE stock or the Super Fox 12-gauge CE for crows and waterfowl, but as the weight of time transferred to the carry, he chose a Parker VH 28, 26" double trigger gun that had experienced a very bad hair day, highlighted with butchered stock and dubious metal that found itself languishing with Joe Cimeno at Atlantic Sportsman.

With the help of the Del Gregos and Bob Runge, it became a BH that he fondly called "The Magic Gun." It suited him well.

So that which began, destined as a-once-upon-a-time fairytale with a usual happy ending, ended sadly, February 27, 2015. That morning, he slipped away quietly, boarding the Silver Eagle one week to the day after I held and squeezed his frail hand ever so firmly, "*So long*," with tightening that signaled remembrance after each recollected memory, his only offer of response, the whisper now failing him…then a stillness befell The Old Pats Society.

I recall a fitting line from Ben Ames Williams on Chet MCausland of Fraternity Village that weighs heavily at this time: "A thing gone, but well remembered, is not lost. Rather it becomes by a sort of compound interest more deeply to be treasured through the years." He has etched a deep mark among many of us…a treasured sportsman, colleague, and friend.

In the end, it is not about the birds, the guns, the most toys, but about relationships, good friends, family, children, good times, memories, and the richness it brings to life. One just cannot make Old Friends, and it is in such times like this when we lose one that the knife cuts deep, as a reminder of those precious days we spent, now gone forever, and with them gone is my best friend of fifty years.

(Back) Jerry Havel, Tom Larson, Lance Wheaton, Chuck Mosher, Frenchy, Allan Swanson, Scott Hanes, Art Wheaton, (center) Tim McCormack, Ken Waite Jr., Randy Havel, Parker Havel, Paul Bergere, Ken Waite III., (front) Ken Berger, Jon Foster, Jim Ryan, Shane Wheaton, Tom Wooden, Bill Hamilton, Roger Lowell

Ken Waite Jr., AKA "The Good Doctor";
Ken Berger; and Rick Robison

Roger Lowell

1998 Old Pats Society with after lunch cigars

Cigar Celebrations

"If you are not a smoker, then you politely decline, but if you are a smoker…then by all means gladly accept the gesture and enthusiastically take part in the celebration." Thus came the advice in *The Effortless Gent* article, "How not to look like an idiot when smoking a cigar." Webster doesn't provide a sketch, but further advice is, don't look like a *noob*…go ahead look it up. At some point in time you may be offered a cigar and you certainly are not a noob and don't want to look like an idiot. Some cigar justifications follow, but Emily Post-like etiquette tips are slipped in to keep you from snobbery.

If the choice of purchase is yours, recommendations are to avoid gas stations and convenience stores, but rather to note at the cigar shop that you are a novice smoker and that a nice, mild, affordable stogie should do the trick. Pay note that the wrapper cover seems to have nothing to do with strength.

But it's the celebration part that counts—you know, the *occasion*: a new child, new home, great football game; or, to a grouse and woodcock gunner, it may be that simple and satisfying moment after that superb, unforgettable morning, afternoon, or day afield, the double you shot, the hard crosser, the three 'cock dispatched in that first cover, maybe that great point by a new untested Setter, the first bird with a new gun, or like me, finally have the courage to try the 28 gauge and find how well it will do the job if pointed in the right place.

Further occasions might simply be the great camaraderie where every-body got action.

It might be celebrating that morning of good shooting along and around the five-or-so-year-old skidder trails that laced the hillside, prov-ing perfect cover for 'cock worming in the soft soil, mixed in with an occasional grouse flush when we disturbed him side stepping between the trails, basking in the morning sunshine. The little brook at the bottom rounded out the character of this cover, while the hard going across the brook due to a very steep incline with granite outcroppings took a pass. Good dog work, comfortable shooting weather, and the occasional interception of lead shot against feathers made the event stand out. Everyone was happy for the action. We don't remember the birds to bag because it really didn't matter, except having had the very opportunity. Then came the chance to pause to celebrate the joyous occasion.

It was lunchtime. The Old Pats began hovering around for a tailgate lunch whereby Ken Berger had brought his little Nexus, two-burner, pro-pane, Costco special gas grill, having prepared that morning generous top-quality ground sirloin burger patties carefully wrapped in tin foil.

"Hey, how do you want your burger?" asked Ken, our chef. Each chimed in, "Cook to medium rare perfection," except for Ken Waite Jr., *The Good Doctor*, who said, "I'll take mine well-done." It was always his way: NY strip medium well-done, bacon crisp, and no mooing left in his hamburgers. These large, juicy, melt-in-your-mouth selections came off the grill into an onion hamburger bun, topped with a slice of red onion, slice of ripe tomato, a little lettuce, and doctored to taste with ketchup, relish, and or Grey Poupon Dijon mustard.

You guessed it. Food often precludes the time to light up. Sort of like the menu set for the often-favorite evening festivities before our regular gun show. We started with woodcock poppers, then grouse piccata with capers and sliced lemons, stewed tomatoes with rye bread pieces, ala Berger, and a simple salad of fresh-sliced tomato, cucumber, onion, and capers.

The gun show evenings are a feature of Old Pats Society fall hunts, whereby we all bring our guns out of car trunks, cabins and SUVs after dinner, when the clean-up is done, to lay them out on the tables for inspection, to *ooh* and *aah*, or the sly *umm* showing no particular interest—the dead giveaway warming up for a sale or trade. It gives us a chance to have the adult versions of "bring and brag" or "show and tell" about new acquisitions, and point out alterations such as new stocks, refreshed finishes, and retouched checkering.

Such highlights became our first opportunity to view a fine Parker belonging to Remington President R. H. "Coley" Coleman that "the Good Doctor" was able to purchase. That, exquisite, high condition, DHE 20, with gold inlays, shipped 10/21/37 to Coley, who used it to shoot skeet and then at Remington Farms in Chestertown, MD, and interestingly with the initials E. R. C. or Ester R. Coleman, his wife. This gun had been in that family since inception and now came into the daylight for another generation. It was time for a cigar.

An etiquette tip from Emily: First cut the cap on the "head" (the other end is the "foot," which you light) to create just enough opening to smoke it comfortably without distorting the cigar shape. It's best to make a straight cut with a single bladed cutter, chopping off the head in one motion and leaving the wrapper intact.

Why is a cigar linked to guns and hunting? Well, it calls to mind a quote from Charles Norris, author, *Eastern Upland Shooting*, who said, "A gun is like a cigar and many other things, if a man becomes accustomed to the best, he will never be quite satisfied with anything else."

We identify with cigar smokers. Eastwood lit up short stogies throughout his spaghetti westerns and other movies, some Italians lay claim to these as Toscanos, some arguably claim Cheroots or Parodi, while one trivia investigator strongly says it was a Braniff #3 in *Hang 'Em High*. We all know the image.

Winston Churchill was forever pictured with his favorite, La Aroma de Cuba. Red Auerbach, legendary coach of the Boston Celtics, lit up his Nicaraguan after each win. Even Jack Nicholson sneaked a classic Montecristo No. 2 after Lakers' games. The weapon of choice for ignition is the unglorified, yet trusty match—avoid the cigarette lighter and a chance of taking on the lighter fluid taste—and nowadays the butane torch is preferred.

Again, great food is often a trigger, prompting light up. A regular, without fail, feast at the Old Pats Society reunion is Maine 2–2½-pound hard-shell lobsters, steamed or boiled for about twenty minutes in large aluminum or stainless-steel pots with easy lift-out baskets that hold the critters. A few inches of water brought to a boil before the group lobster immersion, fired from burners connected to propane tanks, is no secret. A good pot holder mitt is a must; once done, lift the gang from the raging cauldron. Accompaniment of course includes dinner rolls, sweet corn, a salad or cold slaw, and ample melted butter in little dipping cups. Once in a while a side of steamed clams becomes an appetizer, of course with the customary soup dish of hot water for a final last wash of any grit before the butter dip. Conversation is lulled as taste buds are on full alert, then some homemade apple pie with a slice of sharp cheese or sometimes topped with ice cream by Doris, Jo, or Sally being the clincher, just before the gun show. All a sure-fire formula for stories and a cigar.

The stage is set to relax and celebrate. Now another Emily clue: it's not really about a tobacco fix but a way to enjoy the company of friends. Don't inhale as it runs the risk of coughing—hold the smoke, enjoy it, then blow it out. Rotate the cigar to get an even burn.

Lunch is in the field, as I began this epistle, around a little folding table, sun high and warm at high noon, in a well-chosen spot to bask in the festivities for an interlude of remembrance. Alongside a little road outside Longville, Minnesota, out of the truck come fold-out or pop-up chairs for many, a dropped tailgate for some and out from the wood boxes, canvas carry bags, or shell bags come the smoked oysters; Brunswick sardines from Blacks Harbor, N.B.; kipper (whole herring) snacks; Ritz, Saltine, or Club crackers; sharp Wisconsin cheese, and knife—all ingredients for a tasty appetizer.

Last fall we met for lunch that day, in the Adirondacks of NY State. Ken Berger and Tim McKelvey, the latest inductee into the Old Pats Society, packed sliced roast beef, sliced ham, hard salami, liverwurst, a couple loaves of Italian bread, Provolone cheese, Bibb lettuce, Grey Poupon mustard, horseradish, Hellman's mayo, some ripe tomatoes to slice, dill pickle spears, Diet Coke and bottled water, while others brought potato chips, wheat crackers, sharp cheddar and Swiss cheese. Tim was still a parolee of sorts in the Old Pats, as his acceptance was not based on shooting skills, gun selection like a Winchester 101 or a Baker he called Barker thinking it was a Parker, but on his culinary contribution, impeccable after action clean-up, regimentation, and excellent quality of pickled asparagus spears. The midday lunch is not from the closest fast-food or family restaurant but a fresh selection from a deli. Afterward it's cause for a celebration with a cigar.

I am not a smoker. My limited benchmark is with only the Old Pats Society choices as references, except a brief time when a Swisher Sweet or Pierogi seemed cool and within reach of a slim pocketbook after a duck or grouse hunt; it was fashion but did not last. I will submit, the smell of a good cigar is tantalizing at the right time. Breakfast time is not a good fit. Lunch, only on occasion, but after dinner, well, perhaps along with a little glass of fine bourbon, single malt, or a martini, the setting is right for a smooth burning; some suggest a Top Stone or Evermore Connecticut wrap or other quality imported product.

This is not a brand endorsement but an observation that some sportsman find great pleasure in a fine cigar when the time is right. I will admit the aroma at the time of celebration is tempting for me to participate while others pamper the palette, but being just a bystander indulging in the true pleasure of good, stimulating, thoughtful conversation vs. sending a flat line text message, has a distinct special reward. Relish the moment, bask in the glow, and sip slowly like fine wine. It is important.

Alexander "Eck" Walls homestead "Then"

Alexander "Eck" Walls homestead "Now"

Another Old Place

"On Christmas, Fay Walls's dapple gray team, 'Harry' and 'Bess,' would parade through town pulling a bob sled, with jingle bells ringing from their harness, part of the romance of winter. You could hear them coming, having left the old farm and made the turn toward town, singing a sweet melody of sounds from all those bells," said Bud, eight-six-year's young. Yesterday's footprints of those old homesteads, farms, and fields are mostly invisible now, along with the people who lived there, and faded memories remain only with a few old folks who remember... then, that once vivid detail finally drifts away, forever.

The last of "Eck" Walls's old place, the hay barn, one day blew down. A single horse shoe, probably from a pony, was found in the rubble; the remains were then burned. Now, near the rock foundation, a single blooming mountain ash and a few old worm-riddled apple trees thrive. Part of his little, overgrown circular driveway, across the road, remains the only evidence of the majestic Alexander and Annie Walls homestead. Meet Eck, who, according to Bud was "a tall, thin, stately man, 'lanky,' who wore a brimmed hat," and Annie, "slim, shy and stayed to herself, slightly bent over as she walked and 'deaf as a haddock,' but they took great pride in their farm." Eck entered the U.S. in 1871 and became a naturalized citizen August 23, 1892.

Bud remembers, "That old place had a gravity-fed water supply from a wonderful old spring that was piped to the farmhouse. One spigot ran continually and fed the soapstone sink in the shed. The other fed the kitchen hand pump. They once had a beautiful apple orchard, in the 1920s and 30s, with some Russet apples that were yellow and fuzzy like a peach. It was second to none!"

About forty years ago, I hunted along the orchard edge when a gray bird flushed. It flew down along the power line that cut across the property and scaled over the rock wall in direct line with the homestead, heading for a big apple tree. After its wings were set, it ran into bad luck from my charge of 7½s. Birds loved the place. Now, the vestiges of time and an invasion of insects and worms—now free from any insecticide—have taken their toll on the struggling apple trees. These last remaining sentinels are enveloped with hardwood tree growth that has sapped the life out of a once-great cover.

This once-vibrant, old New England farmland has grown up in beech, birch, alder, and patches of red bush that have surrounded many of the remaining tired, scraggly apple trees. That long-ago great store of low bush groceries, apples, and leafy vegetables like clover has been squeezed out of nourishing sunlight. The actual homestead imprint and hill behind it, known locally as Wall's hill, have been sold and is now just a wood-lot. However, my brother acquired the long strip across and parallel to the main road where the hay barn once sat. Now, he has commenced to reclaim it. He bush hogged some, then cut the old poplar and birch, opening it up around a few remaining apple trees to allow grass, clover, and new berry bush growth.

With easily walked, Kubota-made paths, it was just the right place to watch my young, mostly white, black-ticked Setter, "Max," discover a new smell—grouse scent. I couldn't avoid bringing them both, "Brandy" and "Max," and after opening the driver's side door of the old '77 Chevy pickup, they had jumped right in and we had headed out to that old place, just as the sun began to dip into the western tree line. Parking on a tall grassy patch beside the old barn foundation, "Max" jumped out while "Brandy" pitched a fit because of the favored treatment. No dog crates this time; both got special dispensation to ride up front, just as it had been most of the summer. The nose wipes on the passenger-side glass windshield told the story. "Looks like dog nose prints to me," one sport had told me when we headed for the lake to fish.

"Yep," I said, "sometimes I use a little Windex to clean it for my better clients."

After quickly tightening the beeper collar, "Max" began to work each side of the cleared walking trail. It was a great evening, the sun, now shaded by the hillside trees to the west, made for a pleasant walk. Wearing a long-sleeve shirt just to keep an occasional mosquito at bay is part of what it's like in Maine this time of year. We worked in and around two or three old apple trees that left plenty of rotting fruit on the ground. With high hopes to introduce him to a bird knowing he was a bit short on experience, we meandered into the "sweet spot" of this little cover.

Casting to the left, but not too far, he seemed to be enjoying the romp. Occasionally returning to the walking path, I coaxed him back into the thicker stuff, not wanting a habit to form of running the trails. A little further along, he came to my call and bounded up, still not sure why I brought him to such a great new playground. Stepping off to my right in a particularly thick patch where I could see a couple of apple trees about thirty yards away, "Max" followed a few steps and then jumped on ahead as he responded to this new direction. He made a cast to the left with a little snap to his tail, then cut behind the apple trees directly ahead, getting very "birdy." Maybe a little luck was coming my way! Once he was hunting the likely places, I took the easy route and worked back on the trail, moving around the cover to the left; this trail followed the natural edge of undergrowth. He got very busy, casting back and forth, showing a little fire, a good sign of a natural instinct and a sure indication bird scent was heavy (likely left there by birds feeding on a few felled apples). The beeper tone turned to a soft steady *beep, beep, beep,* catching my attention in time to see him locked up in the brush. No sooner had I begun to advance, when the partridge flushed. First hidden by the brush, it then burst out in front of me, close enough to see his wing dip as he banked to the right, presenting a pretty fair shot.

Instinctively I raised my arms, got the right sight picture, and pulled the trigger. *Bang!* As the day drained into the west, a time for perfect reflection on a great point and a fine shot. First partridge hunt of the year…but there had been no gun, no noise, no open season; yet all acts of the play were in order. He was excited over the lingering scent and rushed around with great enthusiasm, not realizing we had experienced a rare, uncommon "shoot and release."

Sportsmen should savor private little places like this, places to feel a gentle breeze that touches the past. Take time to look around carefully, like here, finding a telltale fieldstone rock pile, lasting evidence of the cleared fields, some moss covered, with pieces of rusting metal, maybe from an old car or iron from farm machinery, all disappearing evidence of that other life. In that quiet moment, I reached down and picked up a rock, turned it over in my hands and wondered, was it Eck or one of his boys who touched it last? While pondering that thought, a small, dark cloud of sadness crossed my mind. Most of us would never investigate who had lived here or any such place like this, know what the old folk did, learn of their trials and tribulations, but merely think, "It's just another old place!"

History can offer us rich reward about people and their old places. Most of us aren't famous, just passing through this life, leaving a stone turned here and there. Looking back places relevance on who we are and where we came from. I remembered Eck's sons. Erv (Erving b. 1886), who lived in town with his wife, Jesse, ran a little grocery store with gas pumps and had the only Western Union telegraph connection to the outside world. He'd often come down from his home in his galoshes to open up. Bern (Bernard b. 1888) lived on the edge of town with his wife, Francis, who couldn't hear a clap of thunder. Much like Eck, who had a mail contract in 1885, he operated the daily "stage" from Forest Station, the rail drop, to our then little local post office. I pitched hay for him one summer. Raymond and Elizabeth lived away in Millinocket but had a little camp on the edge of town where they often spent time in his old home town. I bought their little camp from Elizabeth in 1977 and owned it for twenty-five years. Then there was Ivan (b.1904), a good fly caster who fished Atlantic salmon and landlocked salmon, especially in the fall in Forest City. He was a paternal twin of Raymond that I met maybe once; his wife was Irene, but I did not know Fay (b. 1896), who married Grace Wight, a schoolteacher and moved away, nor Elden (b. 1891), nor Edna (b. 1894). They are all gone to the ages now, but their footprints, their lives, and their descendants remain a part of the fabric of Walls Hill, Eck's farm, and our little village of Forest City even as final lingering hints of their presence fade away, gracefully, like an evening sunset or a story's end.

The poet Hone Tuwhare captures this loss of a way of life in his work, "The Old Place." His fitting words ring true:

> No one comes,
> No one except the wind saw the old place make her final curtsy to the sky and earth...
> ...there will be no more waiting on the hill beside the quiet tree where the old place falters, because no one comes any more.
> No one.

Time rushes on, moving faster than a leaf in the current, but on this day, I paused, albeit for a fleeting moment, just long enough to think how great it was for Max to find that bird...and to privately ponder the future, like a sentimental fool, wondering if after clasping His outstretched hand, leaving behind a few tattered photos, my life will become etched in stone, as a permanent fixture lost among others in some little quiet and lonely stone village...Will anyone remember?

Epilogue

Eck and Annie are buried in the Forest City International Cemetery, Forest City, New Brunswick, Canada, across the river from Forest City, Maine. Both Forest Cities united their cemeteries into one around 1900. The entrance is marked with two millstones from the gristmill used in the tannery days. You will find fourteen Walls buried there. Bern's "stage," his 1961 Chevy Biscayne, is still locked in the little garage next to where his house stood. Efforts to start it have not been successful.

Shane Wheaton, "Brandy", "Max" and Art Wheaton

A fine collection of eight Old Pats Society Parker 28 gauges

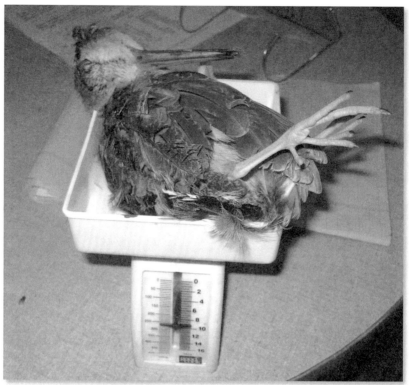

"Sparky" seemed like a clear winner

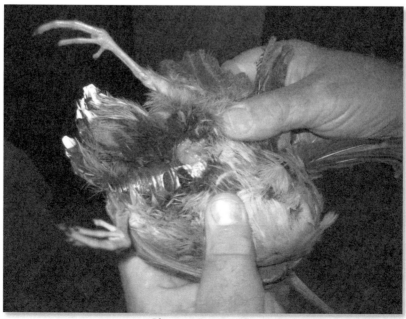

Champion #21343

Sparky

Woodcock Heavyweight Champion!

Old "Sparky" showed up for the tenth round. Nobody saw him coming! When the daily entries were tabulated, each new challenger had fallen short of Ken Berger's first-round knockdown punch of 9 ounces. Little did we know that "Sparky" would emerge as a "dark horse" in the last and final round.

The idea of a prize for the heaviest woodcock shot began in the summer of 2009. The Old Pats Society chef and crack shot Ken Berger devised the plan for a contest, to "weigh" every woodcock shot, with the gunner of the heaviest bird taking the championship buckle.

Scrounging around for a suitable scale to conduct the daily "weigh-in" proved to be a significant challenge. We tried powder scales used for shotgun and rifle reloading, a bathroom scale even, but found them insufficient. Next, we found a little-old, seldom-used postal scale. It became our only option. Confidence improved as the judges felt Uncle Sam would never make a mistake with an inaccurate postal weight! Our scale certainly was not recently certified, thank God, but it was the best choice.

The "heavyweight woodcock contest" spiced the Old Pats Society hunt by providing great animated cocktail chatter. Good shots morphed into great shots with each successive glass of nectar. As the week moved along, the challengers like Tim McCormack's entry of 7 ounces, Tom Larson's of 7.5, and Shane Wheaton's of 7.75 fell by the wayside, and they slunk hastily from the ring. Right out of the box, Ken had dispatched a burly specimen of 9 ounces and our chef began to "strut his stuff." Remember, our rudimentary scale couldn't deal with "grams" so a bit of windage needed to be applied as the pointer bounced around the lined increment. Not only did Ken begin to brag about his pending win and tout his shooting prowess in "selecting" that particularly large "flight bird," but he concluded the contest was over. Somebody passed the spray can of Bullshit Repellent.

Interestingly, one of the most common misconceptions shared by hunters is that bigger woodcock are flight birds while smaller ones are residents. Actually, the bigger birds are females. Quoting my pal and expert, Earl Johnson, Minnesota Wildlife Manager and past coordinator of the woodcock banding program at Detroit Lakes, "Even though there is no set rule to tell the sexes apart using weight, a full-grown bird weighing more than 195 grams is most likely a female, and one weighing less than 155 grams is probably a male, and adult birds weigh slightly more than juveniles of the same sex." Additionally, he says, "The average weight of a bird changes dramatically with the seasons and juvenile woodcock from a late brood will weigh less than birds from an earlier hatch…birds stressed by drought may be 30–40 grams below the norm." I later asked Andy Weik, RGS biologist, for the heaviest-known recorded bird, and he recalled an adult spring female that weighed 279 grams (9.8 ounces) at Moosehorn, while a Nova Scotia autumn female was next at 276 grams. Earl also tells me that, "To accurately weigh birds, a small cloth bag and a good set of scales specially designed for the purpose are required." What does he know about Uncle Sam's good old postal scales?

As our "heavyweight contest" entered the tenth round, time was running out. Just before dark, next to the last day, Jon Foster slipped a nice specimen from his florescent hunting vest. That fine brown bird was brought to the central weigh-in. All eyes were on the scale! The feathers were smoothed as it was laid gently on the postal measure. The needle quivered but stabilized at an even 8 ounces. Close but no cigar!

Only one round/day was left to declare a champion. The next day dawned overcast with a gentle breeze. It was time to pull out all the stops if anyone was to overtake Ken's 9-ounce register.

That evening, all comers weighed in short. No one could eclipse the 9 ounces posted early in the contest. Just as we were about to announce the clear winner and celebrate by tipping our ice-filled high ball glasses with smooth Tennessee whisky, in walked Tim McCormack exclaiming, "Wait just a minute here. I have a nice one."

A rare moment of courteous patience followed. Tim brought his tenth-round contestant to the table. He said, "'Old Sparky' sure looks muscular to me," and with that he placed him gently on the scale. After the needle quivering had ceased, followed by a couple of depressions of the scale so it did not stick, then taking "Sparky" off, then on again, Ken eyeballed the reading. The dust had settled, the dark horse, "Old Sparky," weighed in at 9.9 ounces, the clear winner. A photo finish!

With the hilarity bolstered from strong libation, we paused to salute the "heavyweight champion." As glasses touched, I commenced to retire "Sparky" to the bird cleaning committee. Upon turning him over, a reddened enlargement of the anal area became suspicious. "What the heck is this?" I said. Members of the Old Pats Society gathered round for a closer look. "This bird looks ill," I added. Ken began to probe the red, enlarged area. Finally, after a careful surgical procedure, the cavity was spread open and a large piece of metal began to emerge. A little more persuasion and it was fully revealed…a Champion spark plug, 21343, had mysteriously been inserted into "Sparky's" worm dispenser.

A big cry of foul for immediate disqualification preceded a refill to "tighten up" our glasses of nectar. One keenly observant Old Pats member exclaimed with a touch of sarcasm, "Surely, the only reason Tim was lucky enough to catch up to old Sparky is that he was not firing on all cylinders!"

Woodie Wheaton, author's Dad, "Lucy," Art Wheaton,
and author's son, Shane Wheaton

General Joe Foss, Art Wheaton, and world class shooter
Rudy Etchen in Arizona, 1996

Heroes

We admire our heroes; those who seem to possess great strength, wisdom, and ability; those who rise to the top like cream on new milk, stand out through great accomplishment, are a model or ideal that is looked up to, and who usually choose the right road ahead. Surely, those of us with gathering silver in our hair connect to a number of special, unselfish folks who have distinguished, honorable, leadership characteristics, even noble qualities, and a never-failing moral compass.

Willie sang, "My heroes have always been cowboys...cowboys are special...knowing well that their best days are gone." It might strike a chord with a good many aging grouse and woodcock hunters; those who remember scratchy, weak-signaled, radio programs or the weekend black-and-white serialized picture shows, those thrilling days of yesteryear when we rode the range with the likes of Gene Autry, Hopalong Cassidy, Tom Mix, Roy Rogers, Lash Larue, and the Lone Ranger with his sidekick, Tonto. We admired our cowboy heroes, doing good, shooting bad guys without a trace of blood; we even remember their horses: "Champion," "Topper," "Tony," "Trigger," "Rush" or "Black Diamond," "Silver," and "Scout," respectively. With blazing matched six-guns, the crack of a bullwhip, or the firing of a silver bullet, our heroes galloped across the silver screen and always came out on top, justice always done, leaving us humming favorite old tunes like "Back in the Saddle Again" (*Whoopi-ty-aye-oh, Rockin' to and fro, back in the saddle again!*) or "Home on the Range."

Heroes serve as great moral and intellectual role models of accomplished human endeavor, whose marked lifetime experiences and persona may have molded our beliefs, often shaping our feelings toward certain events and helping us differentiate right versus wrong. They are examples of how we live life and develop the moral principles, the very ethics of our sport. Heroes can be mentors. Some might say our world has fewer of them than in times past, but maybe that's just our place in time.

Baseball gave us Ted Williams, Joe DiMaggio, Roberto Clemente, George Herman "Babe" Ruth, Ty Cobb, Mickey Mantle, Jackie Robinson, Willie Mays and Hank Aaron and a long list of superb athletes. The magic around 90 feet with the crack of a bat, the double play, the home run, or the curve ball, all part of the great American game. It's our game, our National Pastime where we rise to sing during the seventh-inning stretch memorialized at Wrigley Field by Harry Carey's "Take Me out to the Ball Game" (*Buy me some peanuts and Cracker-Jack…Let me root, root, root for the home team…*)

Our men at war produced General Robert E. Lee, Joshua Chamberlain of Little Round top, Gettysburg, from which we remember the "Battle Hymn of the Republic" (*Glory, Glory, Hallelujah, His truth is marching on*), the one and only Audie L. Murphy, the most decorated man in uniform in 1945; Ira Hayes, the Pima Indian who helped raise Old Glory, one of twenty-seven that survived among the 250 who assaulted Iwo Jima; Carlos Hathcock or Chris Kyle, the famous American snipers who gave service "beyond the call" for their country, and my good friend, another proud American, General Joe Foss, South Dakota farm boy and World War II American Ace fighter pilot, USMC, who equaled enemy kills with World War I ace Eddie Rickenbacker.

Withdrawn from combat after Guadalcanal was secured in 1943, a national hero awarded the Congressional Medal of Honor, Foss served as governor of his home state, South Dakota, became a brigadier general in the Air Force Reserve and served as president of the American Football League and president of the NRA. We can stand tall and just a little straighter knowing what they/we fought for, celebrated by melody and lyrics from tunes like "The Marines' Hymn" (*From the Halls of Montezuma to the shores of Tripoli*) or "Dixie" (*Way Down South in Dixie*) or "When Johnny Comes Marching Home" (*Hurrah, Hurrah, We'll give him a hearty welcome then…*)

Our upland gunners of today would be missing a great deal without the rich prose filled with romance and delightful memorable stories from the likes of William Harnden Foster (*New England Grouse Shooting*), Burton Spiller (*Grouse Feathers, More Grouse Feathers*), Frank Woolner (*Timberdoodle, Grouse and Woodcock Shooting*), Gene Hill (*A Hunter's Fireside Book, Passing a Good Time, A Listening Walk*), George Bird Evans (*The Upland Shooting Life, A Dog, A Gun, and Time Enough*), and Corey Ford ("The Lower Forty," "Hunting Shooting and Inside Straight Club"). Their "horses," or tools of their trade, range from a Parker DHE 20, to a Parker VH 20, and a Winchester Model 59. Hill liked to carry his Greener, and Evans first had a Fox but we remember mostly the famous Purdy left to him by Charles Norris. Ford used a Parker. While few remain that knew these folks personally, their enduring words give us a standard on how our game is to be played. They often stand as our role models, having demonstrated lasting sporting ethics, and to some of us, were indeed heroes.

It becomes of little consequence that bag limits are filled, for few of them even talk about the legal allowance of the day. In fact, the measure of the man comes more from experiences like the shot well taken, the bird well retrieved, the circumstance of reward, the rock-solid point or flush, the warm sunny days of Indian summer in glorious October, or just a sandwich beside a gurgling brook with a gunning buddy. It might just be grabbing a half wormy apple from those long-forgotten trees that mark the only remaining evidence of an old homestead, a moment's rest on that field stone wall, that special alder run where the 'cock were on holiday, the partridge that broke from the road edge to find the charge of number 8s a wee bit faster, or the unlikely mixed double when the partridge collapsed and the 'cock appeared in sight at the same time, falling immediately. Special moments live on in our memories.

A good many of us remember such heroes and how they impacted our value system. I can point to a few who impacted my life.

First there was my dad, Woodie, who taught me the passion, care, and responsibility of upland gunning as well as the fundamentals of honesty, good wholesome humor, and putting in a fair and solid day's work, and for that I owe him a debt of gratitude…we only get one, you know. His national acclaim may not be on the scale of Gene and Roy, but as a Registered Maine Guide for sixty-eight years, graduating from the tenth grade with a PhD in the Maine woods and waters, he graced the pages of *Outdoor Life* in 1960, left an island in his name enacted by the Maine State Legislature, had the Woodie Wheaton Land Trust created in his name, and forgot more about fishing and hunting than most folks will learn. He was known for sound judgment and wore his feelings on his sleeve so you always knew exactly how you stood. His skills in the woods and on the waters were legendary.

Then, along the way came Rudy and Joe. That's Rudy Etchen, one of the greatest shotgunners in the world. Rudy and I spent many good times at the Wigwam Club on the South Platte River, the SHOT SHOW, shooting side-by-side at the Grand American Trapshooting Tournament, testing the STS target load in Arizona, in the aisles of the Las Vegas Antique Arms Show, and hunting at The One-Shot Antelope Hunt and The Grand National Quail Hunt. Rudy is an American shooting icon for his never-ending list of wins on the trap line, his twinkling good humor, and wise ability to read the tea leaves and curveballs of life before they left the glove. You better shoot fast with Rudy by your side or the bird you were looking at would already be down. Rudy taught me the way of the fox, to expect the unexpected, consider things may not be as they appear, the intensity and concentration to win at the trap line, and the value of lifelong relationships.

General Joe Foss was a towering presence at the NRA Shows, Western Grand American, and at many a good restaurant. I helped him with his needs for his annual dove hunt in Arizona, often bumping into him on his morning run near the Camelback Resort in Scottsdale.

He was always just regular Joe to me. The general's medal-of-honor leaped from his chest, reflecting his commitment to purpose and accomplishment, illuminating his raw honesty, daring aerial combat scores, his straight talk with no excuses, a resume to prove it, and, above all, words you could take to the bank, a great American patriot.

But sometimes our heroes do not reach national acclaim through known accomplishments, writing, or other means, but can be a good friend, neighbor, gunning buddy, or someone who made an indelible mark on you or showed moral excellence that steadied your ride on the range of life. It might be a grizzled, gnarly, old reprobate who snarls his feelings openly; a patient, understanding, thoughtful, caring uncle, father, family friend, or neighbor who exudes cardinal virtues of prudence, justice, fortitude, and temperance, or other such qualities like (but not limited to) honesty, integrity, accountability, eloquence, enthusiasm, knowledge, loyalty, respect, determination, discretion, or wisdom. We owe them a debt of gratitude for being a guiding light in our lives; they include those who have so enriched the experience as to have elevated the game by demonstrating a reverence for the birds, placed them at trophy status, cemented by an appreciation for good dog work

Heroes come from all walks of life, men and women, patriots who believe in love of country, hard work, and rich reward. We march to their songs; they are our songs: "America the Beautiful" (O *beautiful for spacious skies…for purple mountain majesties…from Sea to Shining Sea*), "America," (*My county tis of thee…*), "God Bless America" (*…land that I love…*), and especially to the penned words of that lawyer from Baltimore, Francis Scott Key, who watched the Stars and Stripes remain flying over Ft. McHenry… our National Anthem, "The Star Spangled Banner," (*O say can you see by the dawn's early light…O're the land of the free and home of the brave*). Their hallmarks are our hallmarks, their stars and stripes is our flag and when it is time "to get those wagons in a circle," to rally the troops, to find that "band of brothers," to look for that North Star, we always find a special place in our hearts and minds for our heroes of this great nation, all who paved the way.

And so…before you hang up your guns, ride that last roundup, hear the music begin for that last dance, or hear that distant drum beating slowly, who will rise as a hero for the next generation of gunners? Paycheck's poignant words gave a measure of importance to it all when he sang about that "Old Violin" (*I turned around and looked in the mirror / And there I saw, an old violin / Soon to be put away and never played again*). So it is NOW, that, *we,* the gray-haired brigade, with more hunts behind us than in front of us, must stand up to fly Old Glory proudly. *We* have a responsibility that goes with these hunting and shooting freedoms, to show others the way, teaching them the ethics, and the values of knowledge, experience, and wisdom for our great American sporting tradition.

We have work to do. There's still time. That duty rests with us.

"Old boy! We have the winning combination for tomorrow."

Art Wheaton collection

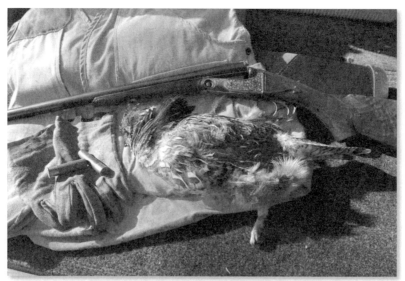

"The Magic Gun"—Parker BH 28

"The Good Doctor" with "The Magic Gun"—Parker BH 28

ONE DAY THE TIME WILL COME FOR YOUR...
Last Grouse

———————————

Such a chilling thought might someday cross *your* mind; probably best we do not know, so, unlike a retiring baseball player knowing when his last game will be, we can't predict the future.

On that partly overcast October day in 2011, the evidence of his health complications became more apparent. I watched with deep concern his loss of energy, the ill effects of his afflictions, as we tackled that difficult cover, the three of us parting alders that grew beside the main road next to a little gurgling brook. We went single file, letting the man in front pick the way forward, then when sufficiently far from the highway, we all turned to our left, spaced ourselves out evenly as we had done countless times over the years. We began moving uphill, still fighting around and through thick brush, skirting a number of blown-down trees, trying to find the best route up the hillside. He knew the drill; no reminders were necessary. I glanced his way occasionally and could see him struggling, unable to keep in line, his effort labored, a signal to pause and wait patiently.

It seemed like just yesterday when those rock-and-roll tunes filled the air: Sam the Sham & the Pharaohs with "Wooley Bully," the Rolling Stones had "(I Can't Get No) Satisfaction," and Martha and the Vandellas imprinted our brains forever with their hit, "Dancing in the Street."

The only noise levels played were *loud* or *louder,* echoing through our barracks at Ft. Dix, New Jersey. After final inspection on an early Saturday afternoon, recruits had free time. Music was blasting everywhere when I approached the young soldier lying on his bunk, just a few steps from mine, reading *Outdoor Life* and *Field & Stream*. I would eventually learn that he seemed to have an encyclopedic memory of the sporting life, sporting collectibles, and sporting firearms, and a liking for some novels like Clive Cussler with the character Dirk Pitt, but it was that great day which became my good fortune, the beginning of a treasured life-long friendship.

Over the course of a long career working together for America's Oldest Gunmaker, we hunted crows at the local dumps of Monroe, Connecticut; the crow roosts at Ft. Cobb, Oklahoma; snow geese at Ile Aux Grues, near Montmagny, Canada; black ducks, teal, baldpate, snipe, et al., using our duck boat and decoys in the marshes of the Housatonic River in Stratford, Connecticut; blue bills (Scaup) and buffleheads from "layout boats" on the coast of Connecticut; eiders from the Rock Islands along the Maine coast; hunted whitetail deer, Canadian honkers and mallards on the Eastern Shore of Maryland, and many, many times, grouse and woodcock in Connecticut, Maine, Wisconsin, and Minnesota. He was there to found the Old Pats Society. Our stories were real, we had lived them all, like old shoe leather, comfortable and well broken-in.

Perfectly timed dry, witty phrases, often delivered from a poker face, practiced from the craftiness of an accomplished gun and antiques trader, he was a pleasure to be around. Like the day he approached "Woodrow," the great grouse and woodcock dog, who pointed a woodcock as he stood in the grass—the bird lifted and after two successive shots from his Parker VH 28 "Magic Gun" yielded an air ball, he offered to the Reverend Leroy and Bill Hamilton, "The grass is too high"; his humor never failed him.

Kenneth Noel Waite Jr., the Good Doctor, loved his "Magic Gun." That Parker VH 28 gauge, with 26" barrels that was discovered about 1988 with a ratty, banged-up, shortened, pinned stock, the metal had about 40% case color and blue but was still in good shape. He rescued the prize from the gunrack of Joe Cimeno's, Atlantic Sportsman, in Monroe, Connecticut, recognizing its potential. Joe said, "I took that gun in one day along with another Parker 28 gauge." Influenced by a fine upgraded Parker C grade 20 gauge belonging to his long-time friend and business partner, Tom Larson, he sought the help of Bob Runge, retired Parker/ Remington engraver and Babe Del Grego of Larry Del Grego & Son, Ilion, New York. The gun ultimately spent many days at the salon being transformed to a graded debutante, scroll engraved with a style that could be ordered from Parker, executed by Bob's talented hands, then outfitted with a brand-new Pistol Grip stock, and forend specifically crafted to his dimensions.

Why was it called "The Magic Gun"? Well, here is the rest of that story. He was hunting grouse in Maine with Tom and Lance Wheaton. The cover was along a field edge, lots of "red bush," Tom on the left, the Good Doctor in the middle, and Lance on the right. Tom recalls it this way:

> We were coming to the end of a cover, a grouse broke hard right going full speed about twenty-five feet in front of Ken when he just threw the gun up and puffed the bird. Lance told Ken that was the best shot he ever saw and Ken said it was not his skill but the magic gun that just zeroed in on the bird. He only had to get close and the little 28 would kill the bird. I distinctly remember Ken was parting brush with his left hand when the bird broke, so he brought the light Parker 28 to his shoulder holding it only at the pistol grip and made a one-handed shot.

From then on, the Good Doctor always referred to it as "The Magic Gun."

Then came October 2012, a day when his passion was still there even though the body was less responsive than it had been in the past. It was indeed essential to dress for the occasion. Very important to be dressed right, like an old baseball player donning the uniform once again or an old soldier with fatigues, feeling the adrenalin of the old days in the jungles or trenches of battle, it was time to suit up: Willis & Geiger jacket, dark green N.Y. Campfire Club baseball cap with the wreath on it, Bob Allan florescent orange hunting vest, his Magic Gun, the green Le Chameau boots he loved, just blue jeans with dark brown Filson chaps-covering. Each article having special personal meaning.

Although slowed from the ravages of Parkinson's and metastasized colon cancer, which affected his speech and stability and sapped much needed strength from the body, the bugle sounded once again. This time confined to a walking trail or an old road, he wanted so much to hear the unexpected roar, the blur of gray, and see the glimpse of a grouse again.

Acutely aware of his dad's inability to negotiate any thickets or uneven ground, the choices to find a bird pretty much had to be adjacent to such a woods road, trail, or path. Earlier that morning, I pulled Ken III aside and said, "Why don't you take your dad and drive down Castle Road, park, then take the little clover-filled road to the right? There have been a family of three grouse hanging out there." Those birds I had seen earlier in the fall and had left undisturbed, in hopes the Good Doctor might have a chance.

Father and son drove slowly down the rough dirt road, watched a moose just off the dirt, in the cuttings, then Ken III parked the black Ford 150 at the top of the hill, just before the road descended to the "lower landing," as it is referred to locally. They commenced to walk slowly down the clover-rich road to the south, with "Trimmer," the English Setter casting about, they worked the right side carefully, then turned to work the other. Suddenly, unexpectedly, "Trimmer" went on point. A large gray bird, startled from an early lunch, hopped up on a granite rock, cocking his head at the intruders. K-III felt it was going to be a tough shot, especially with the bird right out in the open, now on full alert. The bird would have no more of the stare-down. This big mature bird with full ruff—"a 10-point whitetail buck" in my way of thinking—curled away, keeping a wood line of trees between him and the gunner, paralleling the road. It was a hard shot, exactly like a skeet shot, station two, high house. It proved to be a mistake for Old Ruff.

We met in camp later, and when he got out of the truck I asked, "How'd you do?" K-III reached under the Ford's rear bed cover and produced the *finest* grouse I have ever seen. The Good Doctor eased over to me and spoke softly, "*It's been a long time.*"

It was his *last* grouse. It was his *last* trip with the Old Pats Society. It was the *last* time he shot "The Magic Gun." We are now Old Pats minus two.

On February 27, 2015, there was thunder from the throne; another fine sportsman and dear friend was called home. He departed silently, one week to the day after I held and squeezed his frail hand ever so firmly; thinking the unspoken words, *so long*, old friend. We had connected in the eyes and with tightening hands that signaled every remembrance of the rich fifty years we spent together, now so sadly coming to an end.

A clear message…that we must treasure each hunt, for we do not know whether our last grouse is ahead of us or behind us. It is those precious times, those special old pals, and those great stories made together that compose a rich sporting life.

Kenneth Noel Waite Jr., AKA "The Good Doctor," crossed to the better hunting land February 27, 2015. There was no better friend for fifty years. A stillness then befell The Old Pats Society; we are now minus two.

Old Pats Society in the News

Bangor Daily News, Saturday/Sunday, November 4-5, 2006, Sports D7

Shooting sports serve as special friends' bond

Bill Hamilton grinned at the question, his stock answer already halfway out of his mouth. "He's an English setter," Hamilton said, setting up the punch line as he prepared 9-year-old Woody for another enjoyable day afield. "He is the only kind of bird dog there is."

Hamilton later allowed that he was joking, more or less. But on a day spent tromping through grouse and woodcock coverts, Woody certainly lived up to his owner's assessment of the breed ... and to the praise that others heap on Hamilton's top dog when the guide isn't within earshot.

"You may never hunt behind a better bird dog. Ever." That's what many members the Old Pat's Society will tell you, when they're sitting around, swapping tales. *"Fantastic. Unbelievable. World class."*

Coming from the Old Pat's Society, that's high praise indeed. The group of well-traveled friends (along with several invited guests) returned to Forest City last week for a weeklong outing hosted by Art and Doris Wheaton and Lance and Georgie Wheaton of The Village Camps.

Birds were flushed and shot (or not). Yarns were spun. Friendships renewed. New memories made.

Just ask Chris Dolnack.

Dolnack, an invited guest who serves as senior vice president of the National Shooting Sports Foundation, spent a glorious Wednesday with Hamilton and his dogs and did exactly what

JOHN
HOLYOKE

he'd hoped to do.

He continued a tradition.

In the company of men who take their shooting sports (and their shotguns) seriously, Dolnack spent the day toting a gun that was special not because of its pedigree nor monetary value, but because of its origin. "This was my grandfather's meat gun, I think the only shotgun he owned," the Suffield, Conn., man said during an afternoon break. "It's a Savage Stevens Model 5100, 16-gauge."

In a special place, working behind a dog some describe as legendary, it seemed to be the perfect occasion to run the old Savage through its paces.

"He carried it for 50 years and the gun was passed along to me," Dolnack said. "I recently got it checked out by a competent gunsmith to make sure it was safe to use, and came up here to try to bag something with granddad's gun so that I can pass it along to my kids or maybe my nephews."

Though Dolnack isn't an Old Pat — membership in the group is difficult to attain — he obviously shares the group's sentiments.

The Old Pats are big on tradition, nostalgia, and preserving a way of life that isn't as common as it once was.

"I think that's what's so great about our hunting heritage," Dol-

nack said, after bagging three woodcock with his grandfather's old gun. "One generation passing on woodsmanship and ethics and marksmanship and conservation ethic to the next generation."

Dolnack may have shot a limit of woodcock, but if he hadn't, he wouldn't have worried about it. Neither would any of the Pats.

Those days, member Art Wheaton says, are over.

"It's not important to us whether we limit out, whether we kill a lot of birds," Art Wheaton said. "If we make some good shots and kill a bird here or there, it's frosting on the cake. We just have a good time."

All around him on Wednesday night, as a bluegrass band played and steaks were served in Wheaton's beautiful log home on East Grand Lake, similar sentiments were shared by men who sometimes worked together, often hunted together, and who have shared a lifelong passion for the outdoors.

"This is what the tradition of hunting and sports shooting and firearms ownership is all about, as far as I'm concerned," said James Jay Baker. "These kinds of get-togethers have been going on since the first people arrived on these shores from wherever they were from, and probably before that. I'm sure the Indians had the same sort of camaraderie."

Baker, an Old Pat's member, knows the shooting sports well. He spent 20 years working for the National Rifle Association, and now works as a partner for the

Federalist Group in Washington, D.C.

"[This reunion] is very special. You can see it's not about killing as many birds as you can or anything like that," Baker said. "It's about the camaraderie, the shared tradition, the fellowship, just being in each others' company, and swapping a few lies and maybe having an adult beverage or two."

Tradition. Camaraderie. Again and again, those key

> *"It's about the camaraderie, the shared tradition, the fellowship, just being in each others' company."*
> JAMES JAY BAKER

concepts are discussed.

Pass it along to the next generation. Enjoy the time you have. Live. Laugh ... and get laughed at.

Guns brought many members of the society together, and guns still help cement that bond today.

Wheaton and many other members worked at Remington Arms. Several are also passionate about Parker shotguns, and their annual gun show is a key part of the Old Pat's Society outing.

And though they love collecting Parkers, they realize that sharing the tradition of those fine American-made firearms is a responsibility they can't ignore.

A few years back, Art Wheaton illustrated that when he gave away his favorite Parker, a gun he still calls "a grouse machine."

At an Old Pat's Society outing, he handed the gun to his son, Shane, during a special ceremony.

"It was important for me to give it to him while I was alive, so he could enjoy it," Art Wheaton said. "It was more important for him to have my gun than it was for me to kill a lot more grouse."

Charlie Herzog, a tireless retiree from Ste. Genevieve, Mo., is another Parker buff. During his stay in Forest City, Herzog — a member of the board of directors of the Parker Gun Collectors Association — was in the middle of all the festivities.

If there was dancing to be done, Herzog did it. If there were jokes to be told, Herzog told them. And if there were new friends to be made, Herzog was the oneman welcoming committee ... even though he, too, was an invited guest, not an official Pat.

Spend time with him in a bird covert and he'd keep you laughing. Ask him about Parker shotguns and you'd get an enthusiastic earful.

"Artwork is not necessarily canvas and oil," Herzog said. "It can be wood and steel. And a lot of these old firearms that folks like to hunt, collect, and appreciate are just like that: They're works of art."

Herzog was bitten by the Parker bug 13 or 14 years ago, he says. Since then, he has owned several. The hunt, he says, is more impor-

tant than the acquisition. And the people make it all worthwhile.

"You have lots of history, lots of nostalgia, and lots of fun," Herzog said. "And you meet some wonderful people. Those are the kinds of things that make it fun.

Herzog, you quickly realize, is not a man who ever lacks for fun. Those around him end up chuckling, or smiling, or nodding their heads.

This camaraderie thing? Herzog's a world-class practitioner of the craft.

All of which suits Art Wheaton perfectly.

Hunting and shooting have been a big part of Wheaton's life. But the little things remain important ... and spending time around the people who can appreciate those little things is more of a focus as the years pass.

"There is a beginning and an end, and we're all closer to the end than we are to the beginning," Art Wheaton said. "I've said it a dozen times to this crowd: We've got more grouse hunts behind us than we do in front of us."

Wheaton paused and smiled. Steaks were on the grill. The strains of bluegrass music wafted onto the deck. Life was good.

"It's important for us to pass this along to our kids," he said, sharing the message of the day. "That's what it's all about."

John Holyoke can be reached at jholyoke@bangordailynews.net or by calling 990-8214 or 1-800-310-8600.

163

www.bangordailynews.com

Industry leaders hunt birds Down East

JOHN HOLYOKE

After bushwhacking our way through the far-flung bird covers of Washington and Penobscot counties, an enthusiastic group of bird hunters gathered in Forest City last week to talk about guns, dogs, life, and birds.

The Old Pat's Society was back in town, staying at Lance and Georgie Wheaton's Village Camps on East Grand Lake.

The Old Pat's — the apostrophe is theirs, not mine, so please forgive the apparent punctuation faux pas — are a group of friends who have been meeting up each year since the 1970s to do a bit of hunting, tell more than a few stories (some of which we can actually print in these family pages), and eat like kings.

And while membership in the Old Pat's Society is an exclusive honor — being related to a member is a good way to get in, although it's no guarantee — the society also welcomes a few "invited guests" each year.

That's how I gained entrance ... and that's how I met up with the fellows you're going to meet.

Guys like Chris Dolnack, the senior vice president of the National Shooting Sports Foundation, the firearms and ammunition industry's trade association.

Dolnack, who lives in Suffield, Conn., was also an invited guest, and we spent a day trailing behind the eager dogs of guide Bill Hamilton.

Guys like Charlie Herzog, of Ste. Genevieve, Mo., a board member of the Parker Gun Collectors Association you'll hear more about this weekend.

And guys like James Jay Baker, a partner in a Washington, D.C., lobbying and legal shop called the Federalist Group.

Baker was a 20-year employee of the National Rifle Association and now represents the NRA, the National Shooting Sports Foundation, and Safari Club International and had a unique perspective on the challenges facing hunters.

Lawsuits have been filed in Minnesota and Maine to ban trapping in order to prevent the incidental take of lynx. And Baker says folks in Washington are paying close attention.

"Safari Club International, who we represent on Capitol Hill, we lobby for them — I heard from them yesterday while we were up here shooting grouse and woodcock that they had decided as an organization to intervene, I guess on behalf of the State of Maine, who are the defendants of the case," Baker said.

Baker, who has been involved in national lobbying efforts for years, said the emerging pattern is clear.

"The organizations that bring these types of lawsuits — I'm not talking about the specific one in this case — but that type of organization I've been dealing with for well over 20 years and their stated goals are to stop sport hunting, to stop trapping, and they are affiliated with and have interlocking board members with organizations that want to ban firearms as well," he said.

"My opinion, based on my own experience, is that they're not going to be happy until firearms and hunting, and in this case trapping, are done away with," Baker said.

Thus, there's plenty of work for folks like Baker.

And plenty of work for folks like Dolnack, whose group is involved with a variety of projects that aim to show how enjoyable and safe the shooting sports can be.

"Almost everything we do is geared at either eliminating barriers to participation or creating opportunities so that people can participate in hunting and shooting," Dolnack said. "Whether it's trying to get more youth involved through our scholastic clay target program, which is essentially Little League for clay target shoot-

See Holyoke, Page C8

Holyoke

Continued from Page C5

C8 Sports, Thursday, November 2, 2006, Bangor Daily News

ing, or our Families Afield initiative, which is geared toward introducing legislation to get mentoring opportunities for first-time hunters."

"Another important project the NSSF is involved with is Project ChildSafe, in which millions of gun locks and safety kits have been given away.

Coming up ...

In this weekend's editions, I'll take you back to Forest City and tell you a bit more about the Old Pat's Society and their guests.

Art Wheaton invited me to join them for a couple of days of bird hunting last week, and a memorable time was had by all.

There are hunting camps all across the state, and groups that make plans to get together and enjoy the camaraderie in those special places in the Maine woods.

This group, however, is a bit ... well ... different. From its evening gun show to an evening featuring 2-inch-thick steaks and a bluegrass band for entertainment, the Old Pat's Society knows how to have a good time.

Charlie Herzog, you'll find, is quite a character. Art Wheaton, a retired Remington Arms executive who now consults for the company, is still a Maine boy at heart and remains passionate about the outdoor pursuits that have helped shape his life.

And the others you'll hear about? Well, they're pretty interesting, too.

I look forward to telling you more in the days ahead.

John Holyoke can be reached at jholyoke@bangordailynews.net or by calling 990-8214 or 1-800-310-8600.

TV, radio sports schedule **D2**
Harness racing **D3**
High school roundup **D4**

www.bangordailynews.com

Saturday/Sunday, October 7-8, 2006

Sports

BANGOR DAILY NEWS

Landowner makes hunt a success for Bangor teen

Early Monday morning, 1,705 moose hunters (along with their designated subpermittees, family members and guides) will head into the woods to open the state's second session in the split-season moose hunt.

In places like Ashland and Greenville, spectators will flock to tagging stations, some to spy a trophy moose, others to

JOHN HOLYOKE

Hunters breakfast? Let us know

Bow hunters have been targeting deer for the past week or so, but for those of us who use firearms in the quest to fill our deer tag, we've got a few weeks left to prepare.

The residents-only opening day of deer season is Oct. 28, and the season runs through Nov. 25.

First on our preparations list, I figure, ought to be a pretty easy chore. If you're going to wake up in the middle of the night to get into the woods bright and early, you might as well eat well.

As always, there will be a full slate of hunters breakfasts on

Old Pat's Society gets ink

Four years ago, guide Lance Wheaton of Forest City invited me to town for a gathering he said I'd enjoy.

That yearly event, he explained, sometimes takes place
See Holyoke, Page D7

Holyoke

Continued from Page D1

in Maine, but in other years, Minnesota or Wisconsin might be on the group's agenda instead.

Intrigued, I hopped in my truck, headed to Washington County, and met The Old Pat's Society.

The Old Pat's Society is an group of friends — more a fraternity than a club, really — who share a passion for bird hunting behind skilled dogs. Once a year, they go ... somewhere ... to enjoy the outdoors, and the special camaraderie of like-minded sportsmen.

Art Wheaton — Lance's brother — is one of the group's driving forces, and he and I talked at length about the Old Pat's Society, and what the group is all about.

"If you go through life and you're able to count on two hands the number of friends you've got, you've really accomplished something," Art Wheaton told me on that beautiful October evening, gesturing at all the close friends who had traveled to Maine just to spend a week together. "Most people never get one."

Members of The Old Pat's Society (The "Pat" is shorthand for "Pat-ridge") embrace tradition, and spending two days with them was enjoyable ... even though I didn't raise a shotgun the entire time.

And with a distinguished list of members — Art Wheaton is a former vice president of Remington Arms, and National Rifle Association execs and business leaders are also Old Pat's regulars — it was just a matter of time before the group got a bit of national press.

In the most recent quarterly publication of Ruffed Grouse Society magazine, Art Wheaton himself tells the story of the Old Pat's Society in a four-page story.

Wheaton explains the group's origin and talks about the special bond each member of the Old Pat's Society feels for others in the group.

Having witnessed that bond on a two-day trip four years ago, I savored Wheaton's story.

By the time I was done reading, I could nearly smell the gunpowder (as well as the lobsters and pie) that highlighted the first night's festivities.

And I found myself longing for another trip into the Maine woods.

Congratulations to the Old Pat's Society. I hope this year's trip is as memorable as those you've taken over the past 30 or so years.

Warner's work valuable

H. Kendall Warner was a quiet man who was content to let his research speak for him. On Sept. 29, the state lost one of its premier fisheries scientists when Warner died at the age of 78.

You may have never met Warner, but every Mainer who enjoys trolling or casting for landlocked salmon owes him a debt of gratitude.

For 50 years, Warner was a research biologist for the Maine Department of Inland Fisheries & Wildlife, and over that span he became known as one of the world's foremost experts on landlocked salmon management and biology.

You might even say he wrote the book on the topic; three books, in fact.

Warner was a mentor to a new generation of biologists who will carry on as stewards of the state's fishery resources, and even during his retirement, he continued to work on fisheries issues.

As fishing season winds down on even those bodies of water with extended catch-and-release seasons, it's a perfect time to remember all the work Warner did for the rest of us.

Before you cast a fly, before you release that final shiny salmon of the season, take a moment ... think of Ken Warner ... and do something few of

About the Author

B orn and raised in Grand Lake Stream, Maine, with a B.A. in History from the University of Maine in Orono, Art Wheaton spent forty years with Remington Arms Co. Inc. serving in manufacturing, sales and marketing. He rose to Sr. Management as Vice President, Marketing & Sales in 1990 and retired as Vice President, General Manager, World-Wide Sales. His passions include trap-shooting, bird dogs, with a bent for English Setters, and fly-fishing. Art has been recognized as an Industry shooter, winning two North American Clay Target Championships, back to back in 1976 and 1977, as well as the Grand American and Vandalia Championships in 1976, then 18 years later was R/U in the North American Clay Target Championship. He enjoys fly-fishing for Atlantic and Landlocked Salmon and Smallmouth Bass, and collecting sporting art and other sporting collectables.

Art has served on many boards of directors throughout the shooting industry, including Chairing the National Shooting Sports Foundation and Sporting Arms and Ammunition Manufacturers Institute. He is past Chair, 2003 and President of the Parker Gun Collectors Association, past President of the Parker Gun Foundation 2015, now he serves as a Trustee, all of which conveniently justify a few Parker shotguns in his cabinet.

Returning to his youth, he is still a Registered Maine Guide and guides fresh water fisherman during the summer. He's busy having been a long serving board member, Vice President and now in 2015 President of the Woodie Wheaton Land Trust and slips into the thickets in October, before spending winters in North Carolina. Art is a Benefactor Member of the NRA, Life member of the Grand National Quail Club, the One-Shot Antelope Hunt, Bass Anglers Sportsman Society, Ruffed Grouse Society, Amateur Trapshooting Association and Parker Gun Collectors Association. He brings a lifelong interest in hunting across the North American Continent and Africa, but his first love is gunning grouse and woodcock, expending his share of 28 gauge shells in the covers of Canada, Minnesota, Wisconsin, New York, Michigan, Pennsylvania and Maine.

Art is currently a Field Editor for *Ruffed Grouse Society Magazine*, often published in *Double Gun Journal* and has contributed to *Shooting Sportsman, Wildfowl, Echoes, Discover Maine* and *Sporting Classics* magazines. His work is found in the books, *A Passion for Grouse, Classic Deer Camps,* and in the forewords of *The History of Remington, The Art of Remington* and *Field to Feast.*

He and his wife, of 52 years, Doris spend summers in Forest City, Maine. They enjoy their three children, Heather, Holly and Shane, and the busy escapades of their five grandchildren. If you are overrun with birds, quickly e-mail a message to Art.Wheaton@Gmail.com and he'll come running. All maps will be kept top secret.